AQB3903

D0401238

THE
BEST
CHRISTIAN
WRITING
2006

Series Editor
John Wilson

Introduced by Mark Noll
John Wilson

JOSSEY-BASS
A Wiley Imprint
www.josseybass.com

Published by Jossey-Bass
A Wiley Imprint
989 Market Street, San Francisco, CA 94103-1741   www.josseybass.com

Jossey-Bass books and products are available through most bookstores. To contact Jossey-Bass directly call our Customer Care Department within the U.S. at 800-956-7739, outside the U.S. at 317-572-3986, or fax 317-572-4002.

Jossey-Bass also publishes its books in a variety of electronic formats. Some content that appears in print may not be available in electronic books.

Library of Congress Cataloging Card Number

ISBN-13: 13-978-0-7879-7475-6
ISBN-10: 0-7879-7475-7
ISSN: 1542-8559

Printed in the United States of America
FIRST EDITION
PB Printing   10 9 8 7 6 5 4 3 2 1

CONTENTS

INTRODUCTION: GOOD WRITING IS CLEAR WRITING—AND IT'S THE SAME FOR GOOD CHRISTIAN WRITING TOO

Mark Noll

The third chapter of 1 Samuel records a telling phrase describing God's care for the young man who would one day become the prophet for all Israel: "As Samuel grew up, the Lord was with him and let none of his words fall to the ground" (1 Samuel 3:19, NRSV). God is not with those of us who live in modern Western societies as he was with Samuel, for our words fall to the ground all the time. In fact, most of us live amid steady torrents of words falling to the ground: words we generate ourselves in thralldom to e-mail—words crashing upon us in hyperfrenetic appeals to buy, buy, buy—words pouring like Niagara from a vast array of personalized electronic devices—words of several kinds rising effortlessly from ever smaller cell phones—words in print from magazines for every taste—words when we stop and when we go—words with tunes and tuneless. We are awash in words, and mostly they fall to the ground.

Good writing, as in the essays gathered in this book, is made up of words that do not fall to the ground. Good Christian writing, which of course is always difficult to define, possesses an added dimension. Not only do the words of good Christian writing hit a mark, not only do they possess qualities shared with good writing in general, not only do they genuinely illuminate some human situation or human personality—but they do so from a specific angle. The angle is the reality of Christian faith. But how the angle comes into play as written words hit their mark is not predictable. Although an awful lot of formulaic Christian fiction now exists alongside formulaic Christian how-to books, and although some of that writing is surprisingly helpful for laudable purposes, good Christian writing does not arise from the application of formulas. The variety in the pieces that follow—of tone, substance, perspective, temperament, theme, and level of confidence or doubt—should be enough to scotch the search for formula as the key to good Christian writing.

Yet if good writing—and good Christian writing—does not answer to formula, it is still valuable to try to specify what makes good writing good.

Making such an effort has led me to the conclusion that the one essential quality of good writing is clarity. Not necessarily simplicity, though in an age of obfuscation it is almost always true that the simpler is better. And not necessarily instant comprehensibility either, though in an age of gobbledygook getting to the point directly is almost always an advantage.

Rather, clarity is the key, though to be clear may take different forms depending on what an author is trying to be clear about. If the subject is complex or mysterious or profound, clear writing should take readers simply and comprehensibly to that subject, but it does not guarantee that, once engaged, the subject will itself fall neatly into place.

As of 2005, the revised Scholastic Aptitude Test (SAT) requires a writing sample. This test, which has become permanently entrenched in the rituals of transition from adolescence to college, now requires students to write a short essay in response to a set question. Grading the essay is naturally tricky, since hundreds of part-timers (mostly high school and college English teachers) are sharing the labor, and since these graders have been instructed not to mark off for bad penmanship no matter how sloppily the students have inscribed the page during the twenty-five minutes allotted for the task.

It is easy to pick holes in such an exercise, but the guidelines for grading are not too bad. For differentiating among essays on a scale of zero to six, the guidelines isolate qualities that testify in their own relatively clear fashion to the values of clear writing. Here are the standards:

0—No answer or answer not on topic.
1—No viable point of view, disorganized, pervasive grammar flaws.
2—Weak critical thinking, insufficient or inappropriate examples, frequent problems in sentence structure.
3—Some critical thinking but limited organization and focus. Accumulation of grammatical errors.
4—Develops a point of view with evidence to support position, inconsistent use of language.
5—Strong critical thinking, organized and focused, generally free of errors.
6—Outstanding. Clear and consistent mastery, skillful use of language, although it may have a few minor errors.[1]

It would have been ideal if these guidelines were themselves presented in a grammatically parallel form, which would have made them clearer, but they still catch nicely the combination of formal and substantial qualities that make for good writing. For nonfiction and fiction, poems and essays, clarity means mastery of form, of the tools of language, so as to be able to say what the writer wants to say—the better this goal is reached, the better the writing. But good writing also means that well-presented words say something clearly about the subject under consideration. What the SAT calls "a point of view" and "strong critical thinking" must complement the use of good grammar and the spelling of most words correctly.

Philosophers, theologians, and the aesthetically minded could go on to expand upon these generalizations. But for one who thinks concretely as a historian, examples work much better. For nearly every instance I can think of to illustrate good writing, illumination is the key. Clarity of prose or poetic form combined with clarity in showing something real about the object under consideration makes the difference.

The special merit of the greatest living American historian is the special clarity he has brought to every subject he has touched. Edmund S. Morgan, now well into his eighties, has over a long publishing career written with luminous grace about the Puritans, the Stamp Act and Revolutionary crises of the eighteenth century, the tangled fate of slavery and liberty in colonial America, and the lives of early Americans noteworthy for their pathbreaking ideas (Roger Williams) or their service to the new nation (George Washington, Benjamin Franklin). A recent review of a book of Morgan's own book review essays commends especially the ability to make things clear: "[H]e often makes a better case for a book than its author could. I tried several times to grasp the tangled argument of Sacvan Berkovitch in *The American Jeremiad* (1978), but I could not get it clear in my head till I read Morgan's pellucid restatement of it. He makes it not only clearer but more persuasive."[2] What Morgan has done in excellent writing about books he has done even more in excellent writing about the events and personalities of early American history.

An enduring example of Morgan's gift is his short study *The Puritan Dilemma: The Story of John Winthrop,* published by Little, Brown more than forty years ago. The book remains a model of historical mastery, human insight, and lapidary prose. In relatively few pages Morgan could not deal comprehensively with all particulars of Winthrop's exemplary career as the leading figure of early Massachusetts Bay. But he did mine thoroughly the substantial corpus of sources that exists for Winthrop and his times, and he conveyed what he researched with extraordinary grace and economy—for example, "[T]he central Puritan dilemma [was] the problem of doing right in a world that does wrong"; and of Winthrop's death in 1649, "On March 26 he reached what in life he had never sought, a separation from his sinful fellow men." In this as in all of his books Morgan achieved an unusual measure of clarity about a person or situation of unusual significance.

The same combination of effective prose and consequential substance—adeptly deployed for illuminating a subject's life—is relatively easy to spot in other noteworthy biographies. Harry Stout's study of George Whitefield, *The Divine Dramatist: George Whitefield and the Rise of Modern Evangelicalism* (1991), is memorable not only for its insights into how Whitefield's joining of commercial instincts to religious convictions anticipated later evangelical history, but also for the verve with which Stout develops this important thesis. The two best recent biographies of Abraham Lincoln are Allen Guelzo's *Abraham Lincoln: Redeemer President* (1999) and Richard Carwardine's *Lincoln* (2003). They make for excellent reading because these authors have mastered Lincoln scholarship to the degree demanded by experts, but also succeed in opening up Lincoln's extraordinary life for broad and nonspecialist audiences.

Others of this type include Peter Brown's *Augustine of Hippo* (2nd ed., 2000), the best biography of the most influential figure in Western history after Jesus Christ; Adrian Desmond and James Moore's *Darwin: The Life of a Tormented Evolutionist* (1991), the most persuasive account of how Darwin's science related to the politics of his age; and George Marsden's *Jonathan Edwards: A Life* (2003), the most successful effort ever published to describe this supernal theologian against the background of his day-to-day New England life. Such biographies are unquestionably good reading because they reveal their subjects to readers clearly and because their words, sentences, and paragraphs flow with such pointed force to that end. For most of these writers, effortless prose required unusual effort. For all of them, the result was a clearer picture of a person and clearer understanding of why that person was important.

One more, lesser-known biographical study offers an especially telling example of good writing. It is David Newsome's *The Parting of Friends: The Wilberforces and Henry Manning* (1966), an old-fashioned kind of history about old-fashioned kinds of people. Newsome's subjects lived during the first half of the nineteenth century in the circle created by the household of the evangelical campaigner against slavery William Wilberforce. This circle was made up of several of Wilberforce's children, their friends, and their associates, themselves a remarkable group of Victorian women. The plotline is the story of the drift from the sturdy evangelicalism of the older Wilberforce to high-church Anglicanism and then, for some under the guidance of John Henry Newman, to the Roman Catholic church. The poignancy of the story is the combination of intense fraternal devotion and painful ecclesiastical separation. When some in this circle remained Anglican, the result was broken relationships in homes, colleges (most were connected to Oxford), and the church. Newsome's gift is to shape the treasure trove of letters left by the participants (they were scribbling away all the time) into a compelling narrative that, while it solves no problems of theology or church loyalty, nonetheless opens readers to the profound humanity of those who engaged those issues in that corner of Victorian England more than a century and a half ago.

For autobiography, it is harder to say what is being clarified than with good biographies. Malcolm Muggeridge's two volumes of memoirs, *Chronicles of Wasted Time* (1972, 1973), by far the best thing this compulsive "vendor of words" ever wrote, is a case in point. It is certainly a great book, although what kind of great book is hard to say. Muggeridge presented this two-volume work as an autobiography, but it is selective to the point of fiction and strongly backloaded to reflect Muggeridge's opinions as they had come to develop by the 1970s. Doubts as to genre notwithstanding, the volumes are as sharp an evisceration of the modern zeitgeist as one could possibly hope to read. Muggeridge knew almost everyone of note in Britain and also in many other places of the world. As told in these volumes, his life was a perpetual series of disillusionments with the gods of the age (Fabianism, Marxist socialism, Western affluence) and a progressive self-understanding of what it meant as a journalist extraordinaire, even in the most secular of centuries, to be haunted by God. It is hard to imagine crisper prose than Muggeridge presents in these books; it is even harder to imagine a clearer demonstration of what it means for Augustine's "City of God" to infiltrate a "City of Man."

Standards of good writing for general nonfiction are less complicated than for autobiography, or even biography.

Readers want to know about the subject advertised in title and on dust jacket; the author's job is to deliver. Good non-fiction writing, thus, will depend in large measure on the varied interests of varied readers. With a life given over to researching and teaching the history of Christianity, there is no doubt in my mind about the best writing in recent years on "my" subject. It comes in two volumes of essays by the Scottish septuagenarian missiologist, Andrew Walls: *The Missionary Movement in Christian History* (1996) and *The Cross-Cultural Process in Christian History* (2002). In this case, however, the writing clarifies much more than I had anticipated when I first picked up the books.

These volumes must be the best books ever written to show how the worldwide spread of Christianity fulfills the inner character of the Incarnation. As a series of essays, the volumes suffer some from occasional repetition and a few gaps of coverage, but these are minor blemishes compared to the riches they unfold. Walls argues that Christianity, in its essence, is a religion of translation—first the Word of God into human flesh, then Jewish forms of Christian faith into Mediterranean, then Mediterranean into Northern European, then Northern European into the diverse cultures to the ends of the earth. By studying the process of translation—by noting the often very different ways in which Christianity takes root in different cultures at different times—readers under Walls's tutelage can marvel at how God creatively combines the eternal and timeless with the timebound and parochial. Taken together, these books clarify both the course of Christian history and the meaning of Christian theology; they offer a theology of culture and of Christian mission true to "the Word made flesh." It does not hurt that Walls is as witty as he is humble, and that his scholar's eye can synthesize telling details from the whole length of Christian history with the whole breadth of modern Christian expansion. Superb exposition + unexpected illumination = good writing.

For poetry, clarity of a different sort comes to the fore, since the goal is not so much thorough, discursive understanding as sharp, concentrated insight. The best poets (in my prejudiced opinion) of the best century of English-language verse were masters of such insight. In the seventeenth century, concern for authors as subjects of their own poetry was not unknown, but that concern had not swelled to the extent reached in modern eras when poetry has been blighted by a tendency to make authors the central themes of their poems. By contrast, poets in that far-gone age were not afraid to give themselves unstintingly to the task of looking at the most profound realities in order to write about them clearly. At its best, that clarity, though far from simple, has never been equaled.

So it was with the best of these poets, George Herbert (1593–1633), who on many occasions compacted the most basic realities of Christian faith into a single poetic paragraph. In the last stanza of "The Agonie" this task was accomplished for the meaning of the crucifixion:

> Who knows not Love, let him assay
> And taste that juice, which on the crosse a pike
> Did set again abroach; then let him say
>   If ever he did taste the like.
> Love is that liquor sweet and most divine,
> Which my God feels as bloude; but I, as wine.

Herbert's capacity extended beyond an ability to convey the depth of Christian belief to comparable insight concerning the deepest realities of the Christian life, as in this stanza from "The Dawning," wherein he shows the ongoing significance of Christ's rising from the dead:

> Arise sad heart; if thou dost not withstand,
>   Christ's resurrection thine may be:
> Do not by hanging down break from the hand
>   Which, as it riseth, raiseth thee:
>   Arise, arise;
> And with his burial linen dry thine eyes:
>   Christ left his grave-clothes, that we might,
>   when grief
>   Draws tears, or blood, not lack an handkerchief.

Herbert was not alone in his age with such efforts to clarify the meaning of the gospel in verse. His near contemporary, Edward Taylor (1642–1729), was the longtime minister of the Congregational church in Westfield, Massachusetts, where for several decades he wrote a poetic meditation before his church's quarterly celebration of the Lord's Supper. Included in these meditations are some of the most moving statements about the work of redemption ever attempted in the English language. Thus, in one of a series of poems on John 6:51, "I am the Living Bread," Taylor considered the richest imaginable human fare as nothing in comparison to what Christ offered: "Their Spiced Cups, sweet Meats, and Sugar Cakes / Are but dry Sawdust to this Living Bread." The poem ends, as the meditations often do, with Taylor being swept away by the magnitude of God's grace:

> What wonders here, that Bread of Life should come
> To feed Dead Dust? Dry Dust eate Living Bread?
> Yet Wonder more by far may all, and some
> That my Dull Heart's so dumpish when thus fed.

Lord Pardon this, and feed mee all my dayes,
With Living Bread to thy Eternall Prayse.

It was similar with one of Taylor's several meditations on John 6:55, wherein Jesus proclaimed that "my blood is drink indeed." Taylor wrote that, although he was sin-sick—"My Soule had Caught an Ague, and like Hell / Her thirst did burn"—God had provided the most powerful medication imaginable: in his "bright blazing Love did spring a Well / of Aqua-Vitae in the Deity." The result was a bold statement about the effects of that love upon Taylor, but also with reference to God himself:

But how it came, amazeth all Communion.
God's only Son doth hug Humanity,
Into his very person. By which Union
His Human Veins its golden gutters lie.
And rather than my Soule should die by thirst,
These golden Pipes, to give me drink, did burst.

The poems of Herbert and Taylor represent good writing because they show so clearly the meaning of Christ's incarnation, death, and resurrection. To be sure, they pushed the English language to the limit in order to achieve that clarity. But there should be little wonder about the extremity of the language, since the realities they describe, had they not actually happened, would be unimaginable. In their case, the poetry is excellent because it so clearly reflects the profundity of those realities.

So far I have attempted no way of distinguishing "good Christian writing" as a species within the genre of "good writing." Yet it may be that my examples have already accomplished that delicate task. Good Christian writing (a) exemplifies what is required for mastering the forms of fiction, poetry, or nonfiction, and (b) clarifies aspects of the Christian faith. Perhaps it really is as easy, or as difficult, as that.

The prophet Samuel's words did not fall to the ground. They hit their mark. They reached their goal. They communicated clearly. From a Christian perspective, we should not be surprised that God was with Samuel in this way, since Samuel was one of those who, in the words of 2 Peter, spoke "the prophetic message" that has now been "more fully confirmed." That message, 2 Peter goes on, deserves attention because it is as "a lamp shining in a dark place" (2 Peter 1:19).

Good Christian writing makes things clear because it reflects a special light on its subjects. That illumination "gives light to those who sit in darkness and in the shadow of death" (Luke 1:79); it is "a light for revelation to the Gentiles and for glory to . . . Israel" (Luke 2:32); it is "the light [that] shines in the darkness, and the darkness did not overcome it" (John 1:5). Good writing clarifies. Good Christian writing clarifies by reflecting the unique light that streams from the Son of God.

Notes

1. *Washington Post,* January 16, 2005, p. A15.
2. Garry Wills, "Lessons of a Master," *New York Review of Books,* June 24, 2004, p. 12.

PREFACE

John Wilson

If—this side of heaven—you could gather all the writers represented in this book around one big table, they would find all manner of things to disagree about, from matters of doctrine to political affiliation, not to mention whether the window should be closed or open. But what unites them is more important than what divides them. They all believe that the universe was created by God—it wasn't a cosmic accident—and that we ourselves, bags of bones with an insatiable longing for the true, the good, and the beautiful, were made in God's image.

Reality is strange. On this all the experts agree, whether they worship the Triune God, Father, Son, and Holy Spirit, or the Head Quark. The guests at our banquet—the writers assembled in this book—would add that our world suffers from a primeval estrangement. As G. K. Chesterton put it, "there had come into my mind a vague and vast impression that in some way all good was a remnant to be stored and held sacred out of some primordial ruin. Man had saved his good as Crusoe had saved his goods; he had saved them from a wreck."

The consequences of this wreck—what Christians call the Fall—are painfully evident at every hand. And yet, if the astonishing story told in the gospels is true, a crucifixion healed that estrangement. In the face of suffering and evil and boredom and absurdity, the guests at our great feast can raise a toast to the resurrection of the body and the life everlasting, amen.

Christian writing is writing that is informed by this understanding of reality and our place in it, whether explicitly or implicitly. Its natural habitat is the whole world in all its beauty and horror, its clarity and muddle, and its blessed ordinariness. Christians who read *only* Christian writing are trying to wall themselves off from the world—so too those nonbelievers who wouldn't touch anything labeled "Christian" with a ten-foot pole. This collection of Christian writing is for anyone who acknowledges the dilemma of being human.

This book, the fifth volume in a series, was made possible through the help of many people. My thanks to the readers who wrote in response to earlier volumes—and who sometimes suggested new essays that merited inclusion. Julianna Gustafsson, Chandrika Madhavan, Andrea Flint, and the rest of the team at Jossey-Bass were a delight to work with once again.

I would also like to thank Mark Noll, Rick and Elizabeth Wilson, and, most of all, my wife, Wendy.

SERMO CXCVI: CHRISTMAS #13

Augustine
(translated by William Griffin)

Two Births

This very day is the birthday of Our Lord Jesus Christ!

It's a feast day for us!

The Day of days has flooded this day for us with the Light of His Son!

It's also the Winter Solstice. The shortest day of the year. From this day forward Daylight—the light of the Day—will grow longer.

Did I say it was a birthday? I meant to say it was two birthdays we're celebrating today. One divine, the other human. Both are out of this world, I must say! One without a woman for a mother; the other without a man as father.

What was it that Isaiah asked? "Who'll tell of His birth?" (53:8). Was the holy Prophet referring to both births or to just one? Who indeed could do Justice to the story of God doing the generative act? Or a woman doing the virginal birth? The former when there was no such thing as time; the latter on one specific day. Both without human engineering but not without human admiration.

About that first birth.

We find it in John (1:1).

"In the beginning was the Word, and the Word was with God, and God was the Word."

Whose Word?

The Father Himself.

What Word?

The Son Himself.

Never the One without the Other.

The One who was never without the Son sired the Son. He sired Him, yes, but He didn't begin Him. If He's sired without a beginning, then there's no beginning. Yet He's the Son, and yet He was sired.

"But how could He be sired and not have a beginning?" ask the Heretical Hecklers forever among us. "If He was, then He has a beginning. If He wasn't, then how was He sired, since we know He came to be? How? How? How?"

Well, how should I know? I'm only a human being. I don't know how God was begotten. I've labored to find out, I must say. That's why I've appealed to the Prophet. "Who'll tell the story of His birth?"

Now for that other birth, the human birth. Follow me closely, even though I'll fare no better. It's the one in which "He dumped His divinity in favor of the form of a slave." That was how Paul described it to the Philippians (2:7).

Can we wrap our minds around this?

Can we do any better with the previous sentence in the same holy letter?

"When He was in the form of God, He didn't think it a stretch, a reach, to be on a par with God" (2:6).

Who can get to the bottom of all this? Who'll tell the story behind the story? Saying it is one thing, which is what

I'm doing before you this morning, my dear Brothers and Sisters, but thinking it is quite another. Who'd send his mind where no mind had ever gone before? And returning from such a journey, whose tongue could describe what it'd seen? Well, certainly not mine.

So let's just drop this consideration for a moment and return to the previous one. Perhaps there are a few things I can say about it. At least I'll try.

"He divested Himself of His divine trappings, then disguised Himself as a slave; that's to say, He dolled himself up as a human being" (Philippians 2:6–7).

Where?

In the Virgin Mary.

The Angel delivered the message. Kindly the Virgin listened to it. Against her better judgment she believed it. The conception took place. Faith in her soul. Christ in her womb. And that's all there was to it.

A virgin conceives—improbable!

A virgin gives birth—impossible!

After the afterbirth she's a virgin still—too incredible to be believed!

What storyteller—the great Isaiah included—could do Justice to a birth like that?

Three Chastities

Now, my dearly beloved Sisters in Christ, something especially for you.

As the life of the Church began, there were three ways for chaste women to live. A wife, a widow, a virgin. As the life of the Church developed, all three cried out to High Heaven the name of Christ!

First, life as a wife. By the time the Virgin Mary conceived, Elizabeth wife of Zacharias had already conceived, bearing in her womb the herald of this Judge. Wanting to share the joy, Holy Mary went to visit her cousin. The fetus in Elizabeth gave the wall of her womb a good swift kick. The son rejoiced, the mother prophesied. Here you have a good example of conjugal chastity.

Where would we find an example of a widow? How about Anna? Just now when the Gospel was read, you heard about her. A prophetess. One hundred and five years old. Having married at fourteen, she lived seven years with her husband before he up and died. For the next eighty-four she was a regular in the Temple, serving the hours of the day and night with her prayers.

As for life as a virgin, Mary's the premiere example of that.

Which is the right one for you, my dear Sisters in Christ? Wife, widow, virgin? Pick one, and stick to it. If none of them appeals to you, then you're not one of the members of Christ.

Now I know there are wives here today, and I know what you're going to say. "Don't tell us how to behave toward Christ!" Well, I won't. But I just want to say, holy women can have husbands too.

What of you Virgins today? Chaste, and proud of it! Well, you know what Jesus the son of Sirach had to say about that. "The more they swagger, the more they slither. That's to say, the more they crow about the wonderfulness of themselves, the more they should shush their virtues from the public eye" (Ecclesiasticus 3:20, VUL; Sirach 3:18, NRSV).

So much for all the examples of Salvation through Chastity that I've paraded before your eyes. The moral? No one should stray from the straight and narrow.

One last observation. If a man wants to take a fling, he should do so, but only with his wife. Better, he not do it at all. Best, he never wive it in the first place!

Downsizing

What a mercy! The Lord Jesus wanted to become man for our sake. Have no fear. Mercy wasn't devalued in the transaction. How do we know? Wisdom lies on the earth.

"In the beginning was the Word, the Word was with God, and the Word was God."

O Bread of Angels! From You they get their fill. Full plates all around. From You also they get their breath, their Wisdom, their happiness. So that's where You are for the Angels.

But where can I find You?

At the back of a roadhouse. Where the animals are housed. Wrapped in a blanket. Laid in a trough. And on whose account?

He nudges the stars, but nurses from the breast.

He fills the Angels, speaks in His Father's bosom, says nothing in His mother's lap.

He'll speak all right, but only when He reaches the right age.

And He'll fill a Gospel for us. He'll suffer on account of us. He'll die because of us. He'll rise from the dead; it'll be a sign of our reward to come. He'll ascend into Heaven right in front of His disciples' eyes. And He'll come back from Heaven for the Judgment.

Look at how He miniaturized Himself so that He could lie in that manger. That doesn't mean He had to leave something behind in order to fit. He just received what He wasn't while remaining what He was.

Behold, we have the infant Christ in front of us.
Let's grow old with Him.

Presbyters and Perpetrators

I think I've said enough to you, my Charity of Christians.
So many of you here to celebrate the solemnity!

But there's one more thing I have to say, and it makes
me so sad!

The first of January is almost upon us, and you all
know what that means. All those pagan, superstitious
solemnities at the turning of the year.

Now all of you are Christians, and with God's help this
is a Christian city. But there are two kinds of people living
here, Christians and Jews. The Jews are God-fearing people
with sense enough to avoid the pagan pastimes. But the
Christians? Why do the Christians insist on taking part in
these frivolities and think they've nothing to lose? In other
words, I pray Christians will do nothing to tweak the
Divine Pique.

What am I talking about? Iniquity. In all of its forms.
Gambling, drinking, dancing, theater-going. But let's not
rush to local judgment here. No finger-pointing at which
Christian did what un-Christian thing. The Judge of Judges
will be coming all too soon. He'll attend to all of that.

So just allow me one moment to remind you that
you're Christians. Members of Christ. So ponder this! What
a great price Christ has paid for you!

Lastly, a word to the miscreants. Don't turn up your
noses if what I'm about to say displeases you. But do you
really know what you're doing? You're causing all kinds of
sadness and sorrow and embarrassment to the rest of us. Are
the Jews doing it? Of course not. That should give you a clue.

I'm thinking now of one specific instance. It took place six months ago, on the feast of John the Baptizer—a suitable time, don't you think, between the birth of the Herald and the birth of the Judge? The Summer Solstice. A few Christians—I mention no names—went down to the sea and splashed about in some sort of ancient pagan purification rite.

Have you forgotten so soon that John the Baptist had changed all that; that Christian Baptism had changed all that?

I was out of town at the time. When I returned, I heard the sorry news from our Presbyters. They were upset by the sinful way those Christians conducted themselves. Acting in accordance with Church law, they handed out some pretty stiff discipline to the ringleaders.

Of course, as with all Perpetrators, you didn't feel like you'd done a thing wrong. Yes, I've heard your mumbling and grumbling till I'm sick of it.

"It was no big deal, so why are you blowing it up out of all proportion?"

"If only you'd said something about it ahead of time, we wouldn't have done it."

"If only the Presbyters had let out one peep, made just one whisper, we wouldn't have done it."

Well, my dear Perps, if all you needed was a warning, then here's a warning you won't forget!

"Behold the bishop! I'm the bishop here, and I now give you fair warning! My words are meant to advise you, to preach to you, to shake some sense into you!"

And if that isn't warning enough, then how about this?

"This is your bishop ordering you! This is your bishop warning you! This is your bishop asking you! This is your bishop begging you! I call Him who's born today to witness your oath! I extract this oath from you! I bind you with this oath! Don't do it again!"

Well, I've done my duty as bishop. Now you do yours as Christians.

Heed my warning, and I'll spare the lash.

That'll be easier on both of us.

Do heed my warning, though.

You don't want to see me this sad again!

OMIT UNNECESSARY WORDS

On the Trail of Faith and Writing
(From *Books & Culture*)

Andy Crouch

Jerry B. Jenkins is administering the de facto oath of the Christian Writers Guild. Thirty novices sit up straight in their chairs, raise their right hands, and read together from the immortal words of Strunk and White's *Elements of Style:*

> Vigorous writing is concise. A sentence should contain no unnecessary words, a paragraph no unnecessary sentences, for the same reason that a drawing should have no unnecessary lines and a machine no unnecessary parts. This requires not that the writer make all his sentences short, or that he avoid all detail and treat his subjects only in outline, but that every word tell.

We are gathered in a breakout room at the Broadmoor, a sprawling resort hotel in Colorado Springs. There's the faintest twinkle in the eyes of Jenkins and Andy Scheer, the former *Moody Monthly* managing editor who is now Jenkins's writing sidekick, as they recite the words aloud, but the students themselves seem deadly serious. Maybe they are just nervous—each of them has submitted a writing sample in advance, and this is the moment of truth.

Jenkins and Scheer are about to put those samples up one by one on the screen at the front of the room, subjecting each to a "thick-skinned critique." "We're going to leave a lot of blood on the page," Jenkins warns cheerfully.

Indeed, by the end of the seventy-five-minute workshop, nearly every fledgling literary effort is drenched in editorial ink, its adjectives and adverbs ruthlessly run through with a felt-tip pen, its passive-voice verbs summoned out of hiding. The aspiring Christian writers watch meekly. As sheep before the shearers are silent, so they open not their mouths. But when the session is over, they each want their transparencies, edited by the masters' hands.

Thanks to the Left Behind series, Jenkins is evangelicalism's best-selling author, with book sales climbing ever closer to the hundred-million mark. He is credited, variously, with establishing the commercial viability and mainstream credibility of "Christian fiction," evangelizing countless Americans through a tale of rapture and repentance, driving yet another nail in the already tightly shut coffin of Christian literary standards, and exploiting fear for profit. What he has certainly done—though this is acknowledged in tones varying from delight to envy to outrage—is make a lot of money by writing books.

This weekend, though, Jenkins is spending Friday and Saturday—two "thick-skinned critique" sessions each day—wading through prose that would tax the patience of many freshman comp teachers. It occurs to me that, unlike most such teachers, Jenkins could be doing anything he pleases, anywhere in the world. But here he is at the Broadmoor—okay, not exactly a hardship post—with two hundred people who hope that the Jerry B. Jenkins Christian Writers Guild can help them tell their story.

Story is a big word here. "What's your story?" ask the Guild's ads that appear regularly in Christian magazines.

Everyone has an answer to that question. At breakfast one morning I sit next to Steve, a man in his fifties from Nebraska who has spent his career as a stockbroker. A few years ago, he says, God told him to "write my book." It is a book about a thirty-year-old executive who has had everything the world has to offer—wealth, his own Gulfstream jet, his own company—but still finds himself with an empty life. "There will be a lot of water symbolism," Steve tells me; the plan is for the lead character to experience a crisis which leads to his conversion at the climax of the book, a climax which will take place, symbolically enough, in the midst of a flood.

I'm struck by how much Steve's premise shares with many other Christian novels, which gravitate toward protagonists who are at the top of the world's game. What will Steve's hero do after his conversion? Steve's answer is vague. "You know, I've thought about writing this as a three-book series, with this book being the first and the other two being about what happens next." Personally, I'm much more interested in the second book than the first, because I'd really like to know what a thirty-year-old baby Christian with a Gulfstream and a big company would do. Sell the Gulfstream? Acquire his competitor? Steve doesn't know— at least not yet.

The Christian Writers Guild exists not so much to offer weekend conferences as to enroll writers in a two-year correspondence course with a mentor, usually a veteran of the evangelical publishing world. Every two weeks, there is a new writing assignment, followed by detailed critique. Steve speaks effusively of the value of the course—"I bought this course the same way I buy stocks, as cheap as possible." For an $800 upfront fee, Steve has calculated it's only $16 per lesson—a tremendous bargain for someone who gets a personal editor for two years, reviewing, commenting on, and marking up his biweekly efforts at writing. He is a man with a story, just waiting for the time, and the technical skills, to write it.

At the first of Jenkins's and Scheer's critique sessions, I sit down next to Maxine, a woman in her seventies who tells me her story. She has spent her life on a dairy farm in Wisconsin. The past few years have brought the losses that come with age—first her ninety-two-year-old mother, then, last year, her husband, a hard-working farmer who died of complications from diabetes. But Maxine glows with grace, not grief. Her mother came to Christ in the last years of her life. Her husband, one foot turned black with gangrene (she describes this to me in some detail), died in her arms, old and full of years and faith. Somehow in the midst of this ordinary life Christ has become radiantly present, and she is here to learn how to convey his presence in print.

For a few minutes, basking in her midwestern grandmotherly warmth, there is no one I would rather listen to than Maxine. I thank her for telling me her story, and I wish her well in her writing. Yet in my heart of hearts I know that no amount of Strunk and White, however rigorously applied, will get a story of a dying dairy farmer with a gangrenous foot published. The fiercely competitive world of magazines and books—even the relatively friendly backwater of the evangelical publishing industry—not only omits unnecessary words, it must also omit unnecessary stories, stories that have been told a thousand times. Later I tell a friend and editor about Maxine and the story she wants to tell. "Yes," he says, "every Christian magazine gets piles of those submissions, stories of loved ones who have died. Sometimes they're quite moving—I remember working through a few dozen and by the end I was in tears. But we couldn't use any of them."

During a break after the second workshop session I sit down with Jenkins and Scheer. Jenkins is tired—"I didn't sleep at all last night; when your name is on the event there's a tremendous sense of responsibility"—and I haven't asked for much of his time, but he ends up speaking with me for nearly an hour. I comment—gingerly—on the low quality of the writing that students are bringing to the conference. "Pretty thin stuff, isn't it?" he says. Why spend so much of his time on remedial matters? How much do these writers really have in common with C. S. Lewis and Dorothy Sayers, who appear in the Christian Writers Guild's ads? "We're very careful not to overpromise in our ads," Jenkins says. "We never say you'll be published if you just take our course. We do say you'll learn the tools of the trade, and if you stick with it you'll improve as a writer—whatever level you start from. Beginning writers face so much rejection anyway. We don't want to shatter people's dreams. I don't want to be the one who tells someone, 'You can't be a writer.'"

Jenkins has a biblical model in mind—the parable of the talents. "If someone is a one-talent writer, we'll work with them to double that talent. If they're a five-talent writer, we'll work with them too. Good writing is needed at all levels—I don't want to shortchange the school-cafeteria worker who may only write letters to the editor of her local paper." As for putting C. S. Lewis in the ads, "Well, it was either C. S. Lewis or me, and it sure wasn't going to be me."

Even more gingerly, I bring up the question of Jenkins's own work, which for all its adherence to the dicta of Strunk and White—Jenkins's sentences are indeed pared to the bone and his prose clips along at a pace that ranges from brisk to breakneck—has not been widely hailed for its literary merits. "I really admire literary writers," he says. "I'm not smart enough to be one. I don't even feel smart enough to read some of them. I feel like I'm a fairly typical person. I write for myself—I write what I would want to read."

Jenkins's humility seems too unvarnished to be feigned. This is evangelicalism, I remind myself—our heroes are ordinary people, all the way down, who somehow manage to be ordinary in an extraordinary way. Only someone as extraordinarily ordinary as Jenkins could sell millions of books and then stay up all night thinking about how to serve "one-talent" writers. Once and only once during the thick-skinned critique, a genuinely lovely piece of writing appeared on the screen: "Leaves lacquer the Arkansas landscape," it began. Jenkins turned to its author and said, "I wish I could write like this."

But what about developing his own talents? Jenkins has published at least one novel that tries to go in a different direction from his most popular work: *'Twas the Night Before*, a love story that turns on the existence of Santa Claus. But after sixty million copies of Left Behind, he has difficult choices to make. "I feel some sympathy for the college freshman who is playing basketball and is approached by an NBA team offering a multimillion dollar contract. It might be better for him to get a few more years in school. But should he go on playing college ball, risking his ankles, his knees, while that offer is available?"

So Jenkins has decided to leverage his financial success and cultural clout to invest in other people—not just the Christian Writers Guild, which "isn't making me any money," he says wryly, but the Hollywood production company he founded with his son, Dallas. "My son thinks the way you do," he tells me. "He says, well, why not just write what you want to write and let it sell one hundred thousand copies instead of a million?" (The anguished sound you hear is the legions of writers who have written exactly what they want to write and are hoping to sell a tenth of what Jenkins can on a bad day.) "But I ask him, do you want to keep making movies? That takes a lot of money." Publishers can lose interest awfully quickly when zeroes start dropping from the projected sales of a title. What responsibility, Jenkins seems to be asking, do I have to make the most of my opportunities? Jerry B. Jenkins, too, must omit unnecessary words.

⚘

Several months later, I'm at the Calvin Festival of Faith and Writing, a very different sort of conference. The vast auditorium of Sunshine Community Church is nearly filled: two thousand people listening to Joyce Carol Oates, one of the rare literary novelists whose output is comparable to Jenkins's. Her opening remarks strongly suggest that she has never been inside a megachurch before, or indeed been inside a church of any sort for quite a long time. But the festival, a biennial fixture of the Grand Rapids springtime since 1990, has a track record of inviting surprising headliners alongside more predictable names.

This year the crowds gather for children's author Katherine Paterson, for Minnesotan novelist Leif Enger, preacher and writer Barbara Brown Taylor, Oprah pick Bret Lott, and—with especially reverential attention, on the final night—Frederick Buechner, who comes onstage looking like a bemused hound dog but concludes his talk with a transcendent valediction forbidding mourning. During the day, the festival offers a bewildering array of concurrent sessions. Lauren Winner, author of the candid memoir *Girl Meets God*, discusses the perils of candid memoirs; Mark Pinsky, a self-described "left-wing secular Jew" who covers religion for the Orlando *Sentinel,* plays spiritual clips from *The Simpsons;* literary funeral director Thomas Lynch explores "metaphors of mortality." Authors of all sorts are celebrities at this festival, signing books, answering questions, and meeting admirers who want to tell them how their books changed their lives. Enger, looking somewhat overwhelmed, tells me, "I feel like I've been spending the whole conference saying, 'Thank you. Thank you.'" One can even meet that rarest of all literary species at the Calvin festival: the working poet.

Evangelical Christianity, as the mainstream media are woefully slow to understand, is a many-splendored thing. It is a long way from Jerry B. Jenkins's writers-in-training to the world of Calvin College, a Christian Reformed school that is the intellectual heart of what may be the last distinct European-American ethnic culture.

At the Calvin festival, for one thing, I am surrounded by young people. Trim and tall and blond, they throng the workshop sessions and plenary addresses. Some of them are Calvin students who may be attending under professional duress, but most are out of college. There is almost nowhere in the balkanized world of American culture, not to mention American Christianity, where you can find an even distribution of ages from twenty to seventy, but here you can. It's not hard to look out over the audience and imagine a thousand children who "could actually be disciplined," as pastor and writer James Emery White recalls his own childhood, "with the threat of 'no library for a week.'" There's something unsettling about seeing so many young adults intent on listening and reading. Shouldn't they be home, I find myself thinking, watching television?

And then there are books—stacks and stacks of books at the tables of dozens of publishers and at least three conference bookstores. Festivalgoers throng the aisles of the exhibit hall, talking, buying, reading. In Colorado Springs, there were—I counted—thirty-five books for sale. Sixteen were by Jerry B. Jenkins. What everyone at the Christian Writers Guild had in common is that they all were, or wanted to be, writers. But what everyone has in common at the Calvin Festival is that they are all readers.

Is it possible to be a writer without being a reader? Yes—but probably not a good one. There were a few readers at the Christian Writers Guild—the author of the passage that elicited Jerry Jenkins' praise, a retired attorney named Mal King, gave me a slim book by Eudora Welty after we shared an animated lunchtime conversation about southern fiction. But many members of the Christian Writers Guild, coming to writing late in life, have missed something some of us were graced with early on, not even knowing it was grace: books, and books, and more books.

As Joyce Carol Oates speaks, I notice the two people in front of me, both young women—teenagers? college students?—leaning forward, laughing at Oates's stream-of-consciousness jokes, listening intently to her poems, nodding when she mentions her novel *We Were the Mulvaneys.* Is there anywhere on the planet where you could find two people more palpably in love with books and words than these two? After the talk I find out their names and a bit of their stories. Sarah Carleton, two years out of Geneva College and now an English teacher at Beaver County Christian School in western Pennsylvania, has brought along Laryssa Joseph, the star student in her junior English class. "My friends are smart," Laryssa says, "but they don't read, except for class. But I can't go to sleep until I read a book."

What were they looking for? What have they found here? "I think we came because we were looking for depth—something more than you usually find in Christian writing," Laryssa says. "And every session has been amazing. These writers are genuine. They are deep. They are truthful. I think that's what I'm looking for when I read— a writer who is truthful."

✻

Joyce Carol Oates's voice wavers between the tony flatness cultivated by NPR commentators and an unguarded, New Jersey–inflected hilarity, and her thoughts ramble unsteadily, yet somehow believably, from topic to topic. She is talking about teaching Princeton students to write. I tell them, she says, to go out into the world and look at other people. Don't tell your own story—most writers have boring lives. And even if you tell your own story once, whose story are you going to tell the next time? Tell someone else's story.

Suddenly I'm thinking about Maxine, whose husband died in her arms. I wonder if, deep down, Maxine really wants to be a writer. For all of us who write, even for Jerry B. Jenkins or Joyce Carol Oates, writing is work, sometimes deeply satisfying but also draining and at times tedious. Words have not escaped the curse that lies on human work—in fact, most days, most writers will tell you that words are the most stubbornly cussed things of all. To their credit, the Christian Writers Guild doesn't try to convince their students otherwise—many of their students drop out, Andy Scheer tells me, when they realize how hard they are expected to work. And all writers eventually run up against the stark limits of talent: the things we will never be able to say no matter how hard we try, because we simply weren't made to say them. Not many of us get to be C. S. Lewis. Or even Jerry B. Jenkins.

But Maxine has a story, and she's right to want it to be told. It's a true story—no less true for resembling a thousand others. And it's not completely ordinary—that black, gangrenous foot is something you don't hear about every day, even if you're glad you don't. Someone, I think, could tell that story. Someone could make something remarkable out of it, something that would last and matter. Something truthful.

I look across the auditorium at the faces of two thousand readers and writers, and I wonder whom I could introduce to Maxine. Could it be, someday, Laryssa?

It will have to be someone who will omit unnecessary words.

It will have to be someone who knows that no words are, in the long run, unnecessary.

PHIL'S SHADOW

The Lessons of Groundhog Day

(From *Touchstone*)

Michael P. Foley

Last December the *New York Times* ran an intriguing article about a Museum of Modern Art movie series on film and faith. What attracted the *Times* to the series was not its pageant of grave Swedish cinema but its opening feature, the 1993 romantic comedy *Groundhog Day.* The curators, polling "critics in the literary, religious and film worlds," found that the movie "came up so many times that there was actually a squabble over who would write about it in the retrospective's catalog."

The movie, the article went on to observe, "has become a curious favorite of religious leaders of many faiths, who all see in *Groundhog Day* a reflection of their own spiritual messages." A professor at NYU shows it in her classes to illustrate the doctrine of *samsara* (the endless cycle of rebirth Buddhists seek to escape), while a rabbi in Greenwich Village sees the film as hinging on *mitvahs* (good deeds). Wiccans like it because February 2nd is one of the year's four "great sabbats," while the Falun Dafa sect uses the movie as a lesson in spiritual advancement.

Deciphering which, if any, of these interpretations is correct is no easy task, especially since the director and cowriter of the film, Harold Ramis, has ambiguous religious beliefs (he is an agnostic raised Jewish and married to a Buddhist). The commentators also seem wedded to a single hermeneutical lens, forcing them to ignore contradictory data.

A more fruitful approach, I suggest, would involve following all of the clues, clues that lead not only to religion but also to the great conversation of philosophy. Once we do so, *Groundhog Day* may be seen for what it is: a stunning allegory of moral, intellectual, and even religious excellence in the face of postmodern decay, a sort of Christian-Aristotelian *Pilgrim's Progress* for those lost in the contemporary cosmos.

Typical Modern

Groundhog Day is the story of Phil Connors, an obnoxious weatherman at a Pittsburgh TV station who must cover the celebration of Groundhog Day in rural Punxsutawney, Pennsylvania. Phil (masterfully played by Bill Murray) is egotistical, career-driven, and contemptuous of his fellow man. "People are morons," he tells his producer Rita, played by an adorable Andie MacDowell. "People like blood sausage." Phil, in other words, is the typical product of modernity, the bourgeois man who lives for himself in the midst of others. Rita describes him—and us—well by quoting Sir Walter Scott's "There Breathes the Man":

> The wretch, concentred all in self,
> Living, shall forfeit fair renown,
> And, doubly dying, shall go down
> To the vile dust, from whence he sprung,
> Unwept, unhonoured, and unsung.

By refusing to die to himself, Phil and those like him are doomed to die doubly, triply, innumerably.

The Punxsutawney celebration of Groundhog Day culminates with the town elders consulting a real woodchuck, also named Phil, about the next six weeks. The groundhog sees his shadow, an omen that more winter is to come.

Connors cannot wait to return to Pittsburgh, but trapped by a blizzard (which he failed to predict), he and the crew must stay another night in Punxsutawney. When he awakes the next morning, Phil discovers to his dismay that it is February 2nd—again. The same thing happens the next day, and the next. For reasons that are never made clear, Phil is condemned to live Groundhog Day over and over.

Phil's situation is unique, yet the movie hints that it is not unrelated to our own quotidian lives. Commiserating with two locals over beers, Phil asks, "What would you do if every day was the same, and nothing you did ever mattered?" The men's faces grow solemn, and one of them finally belches, "That about sums it up for me." Phil's preternatural plight bears a twin resemblance to ours: first, as a symbol for the Fall, with its "doubly dying" estrangement from God and return to the vile dust from whence we sprang; and second, as a symbol for life in the wake of postmodern philosophy.

For the great father of this philosophy is Nietzsche, and the idea that frightened him most was "the eternal recurrence of the same," *i.e.*, that even the superior human being must bear the same dreary existence an infinite number of times. Like us, Phil is the modern man who must now confront the hardship of postlapsarian life on the one hand and the metaphysical meaninglessness of postmodern thought on the other.

Indeed, Phil's various reactions to his enslavement read like the history of philosophy in reverse. Phil is shocked at his own impotence, so much faith had he put in his meteorological training. ("I *make* the weather!" he tells an unconvinced state trooper.) Phone lines and automobiles prove useless, as do his visits to a doctor and a therapist. All of the Enlightenment's societal buttresses—technology, natural science, and social science—collapse under the weight of a problem outside the parameters of space and time.

Failure and Happiness

Once Phil realizes that in his Nietzschean quagmire there are no consequences to his actions, he also experiences modern philosophy's liberation from any sense of eternal justice. "I am not going to play by their rules any longer," he gleefully announces. His reaction epitomizes Glaucon's argument in Plato's *Republic*. Remove the fear of punishment, Glaucon argued, and the righteous will behave no differently than the wicked. Nineteen hundred years later, Machiavelli, arguably the father of modern philosophy, elevated this view to a philosophical principle.

And Phil embodies it perfectly: Once he learns that he can get away with anything he wants, he becomes Machiavelli's prince. He unhesitatingly steals money from a bank, coldcocks a life insurance agent, and seduces an attractive woman.

To Phil's surprise, however, this life of instant gratification proves unfulfilling, leading him to set his sights on Rita, his beautiful and wholesome coworker. The name "Rita," I contend, tells us something about the role she plays in Phil's life. Rita is short for Margarita, the Latin word for "pearl." To Phil, Rita is the pearl of great price. We know from Matthew's Gospel that this pearl is the kingdom of Heaven, but it may also be appropriate to think of it as happiness, since, according to Aristotle, happiness is that toward which everything in our life is ordered.

And so the overriding question of the story becomes clear: What will it take to attain true happiness? What will it take to buy the pearl?

Phil's initial attempts to win Rita again betray his Machiavellian instincts. Machiavelli contended that it is better for a prince to appear to be virtuous—which fosters in others a gullible trust—than to be virtuous, which hamstrings his actions. And so Phil goes to extraordinary lengths to learn about Rita's aspirations and then to feign the same. (The logic here is also Hegelian: Injustice is justified in the name of historical progress.) Yet the ruse never works; each night ends with Phil receiving a slap in the face rather than acquiescence to his overtures. The pearl of happiness, it turns out, cannot be bought with counterfeit money.

Phil's failures lead to despair. At the end of his rope, he now commits suicide—over and over. Yet no matter how often he jumps off buildings or electrocutes himself, he still wakes up to another Groundhog Day. His poignant awareness of his emptiness recalls the chilling line from St. Augustine's *Confessions:* "I went far from you, my God, and I became to myself a wasteland." Liberation from the divine law initially sounds thrilling, but such freedom proves to be not only hollow, but self-squandering annihilation. As Phil says, "I've killed myself so many times, I don't even exist anymore."

And so Phil, with nowhere else to go, unconsciously turns from modern philosophy, with its "concentred" individualism, to ancient philosophy, with its praise of the just life as the best way to live. Phil begins pursuing excellence (which in Greek is the same word as virtue), not for any ulterior motive but because he *enjoys* it. In good Aristotelian fashion, he cultivates moral virtues (e.g., saving a choking victim), intellectual virtues (reading Chekhov), and a proficiency in the arts (playing the piano). And thus Phil starts to become happy, for he is now fulfilling the conditions of happiness identified by the moralists of antiquity: knowing, doing, and loving the good.

Not God

One can also argue that there is a theological dimension to Phil's transformation. Part of his conversion involves recognizing that there is a God and he is not it. Like most moderns, Phil thinks of himself as (in Freud's immortal phrasing) "a prosthetic god," someone who "makes the weather" through his mastery of science. Later, after his unsuccessful suicides, he tries to convince Rita that he is a god, a claim she rejects on account of her "twelve years of Catholic school" (this is the only time in the movie a religion is explicitly mentioned).

But Phil's conviction evaporates once he is forced to acknowledge the inevitable death of an old beggar whose life he repeatedly tries to save. In the final scene of this subplot, he is kneeling down, vainly administering CPR to the man, when he stops and plaintively looks heavenward. And in an unrelated moment, he indirectly acknowledges God as Creator by reciting the verse, "Only God can make a tree." God alone, Phil learns, is the Lord of life and death.

And then there is the pearl. On what ends up being the cycle's last day, Rita is mesmerized by Phil's now luminous character. As the first item for sale at a fundraising event in which eligible bachelors are auctioned to the highest bidder, Phil generates tremendous interest from the town's ladies, but Rita grandly outbids them all by offering the contents of her checking account. In a happy peripety, rather than Phil buying the pearl with everything he has, the pearl buys him with everything she has.

Like grace, Rita comes to Phil as a freely given gift; like the kingdom of Heaven, she confers on him an ineffable bliss. Rita's purchase of Phil is literally a redemption or buying back from the slave block. (As she coos to him later, "You're mine; I own you.")

It is only after this redemption that Phil—and Rita—wake up the following day on February 3rd. The seemingly endless recurrence of the same has been broken by a love born of virtue, and the couple is now free to live happily ever after. (Because the cycle is broken by the consummation of love and desire rather than the abandonment of it, the story cannot be seen as an allegory for Eastern religious thought. And because this "eternal" recurrence is terminated by love and classical virtue, it is a refutation rather than an endorsement of Nietzsche.)

Though Phil and Rita's romance is essential to the plot, it is not, however, the only gauge of progress. Throughout the movie, the groundhog seems to function as Phil's non-human doppelganger. Both are weathermen and they share the same name. Phil suspects a link but wrongly concludes that as long as Phil the groundhog sees his shadow, he will be doomed to relive February 2nd. (This initiates a tragicomic incident in which he kills himself and the groundhog.) But what we eventually come to realize is that it is not Phil the groundhog's shadow that proves crucial, it is Phil the man's. As long as Phil wakes up in the morning and sees his shadow, there will be for him more winter, more of the same. But if he awakes without a shadow, he will be given spring, a new life.

What is Phil Connors's "shadow"? It is his vices, his bad habits and sinful ways that detract from and diminish his God-given goodness. The equation of shadow with vice is apposite, since both are, in St. Augustine's terms, a privation: Shadows are a privation of light, and evil and vice are a privation of the good. Significantly, when one of the townies hears Phil Connors's name, he teases him with the admonition, "Watch out for your shadow there, pal!" And significantly, the townie's name is Gus—short, of course, for Augustine.

I should add, though, that the movie is not perfect. Rita's final "redemption" of Phil, for instance, results in their sleeping together the next morning. (Call it the incense that had to be thrown on the Hollywood fire.) Also, despite promising hints, Phil's turn to God is underdeveloped and falls short of a full religious conversion.

Purifying the Ground

Nonetheless, *Groundhog Day* exemplifies genuine progress, from the nadir of contemporary thought to the apex of classical philosophy, from depravity to virtue, from wretchedness to happiness. And perhaps more interestingly, the movie taps into a Christian symbol of which its makers were no doubt unaware.

February 2nd in the liturgical calendar is the Feast of the Purification of the Virgin Mary, the feast that commemorates the presentation of her Son in the Temple forty days after his birth. It was on this occasion that the aged Simeon declared the infant Jesus a "light for the revelation of the gentiles." Traditionally, candles are blessed on the feast, with a prayer that "just as visible fire dispels the *shadows* of the night, so may invisible fire, that is, the brightness of the Holy Spirit, free us from the blindness of every *vice*."

Simeon's prophecy led to a folk belief that the weather of February 2nd had a prognostic value. If the sun shone for the greater part of the day, there would be forty more days of winter, but if the skies were overcast, there would be an early spring. The badger was added later in Germany, but the Germans who emigrated to Pennsylvania could only find what native Americans in the area called a *wojak,* or woodchuck. Since the Indians considered the groundhog a wise animal, it seemed only natural to appoint him, as we learn in the movie, "Seer of Seers, Sage of Sages, Prognosticator of Prognosticators."

The ground of Groundhog Day, in other words, is Catholic. And just as our secular celebration of the day unwittingly echoes a deeper truth about the Light revealed to the gentiles, so too does the movie unwittingly point the way back to that truth. And who knows, perhaps Rita, with her twelve years of Catholic school, knew this all along.

SPIRITUALITY FOR ALL THE WRONG REASONS

An Interview with Eugene Peterson

(From *Christianity Today*)

Mark Galli

Eugene Peterson had a publishing life before *The Message*. And one could argue that it was his previous publications that led, at least in part, to the renewal of Christian spirituality among pastors and laypeople today. In such books as *Five Smooth Stones for Pastoral Work, Run with the Horses, A Long Obedience in the Same Direction: Discipleship in an Instant Society,* and *The Contemplative Pastor: Returning to the Art of Spiritual Direction,* Peterson exposed the shallowness of American Christianity and offered a bracing and invigorating alternative.

It is momentous, then, that Peterson has returned to writing about the Christian life with *Christ Plays in Ten Thousand Places: A Conversation in Spiritual Theology* (Eerdmans, 2005). It is the first of a projected five-volume series in which Peterson will systematically pull together themes he has been talking about for three decades—spiritual formation, Scripture, leadership, the church, pastoring, spiritual direction.

The first volume is a tour de force in spiritual theology, combining incisive cultural analysis and biblical exposition with a sweeping and engaging vision of the Christian life.

All of his writing has emerged out of his work as a pastor, mostly at Christ Our King Presbyterian Church in Bel Air, Maryland, a Baltimore suburb. He was the founding pastor of the church, which grew to some five hundred members before he left after twenty-nine years. He went from there to Pittsburgh Theological Seminary and then to Regent College in Vancouver, British Columbia. He is now "retired," living in his home state of Montana, but he remains at heart a pastor who cares deeply about the Christian life as it is lived in the local church.

As Peterson was finishing the manuscript of *Christ Plays in Ten Thousand Places*, *Christianity Today* managing editor Mark Galli spoke with him about themes that emerged from the book and his life.

What is the most misunderstood aspect of spirituality?

That it's a kind of specialized form of being a Christian, that you have to have some kind of in. It's elitist. Many people are attracted to it for the wrong reasons. Others are put off by it: *I'm not spiritual. I like to go to football games or parties or pursue my career.* In fact, I try to avoid the word.

Many people assume that spirituality is about becoming emotionally intimate with God.

That's a naïve view of spirituality. What we're talking about is the Christian life. It's following Jesus. Spirituality is no different from what we've been doing for two thousand years just by going to church and receiving the sacraments, being baptized, learning to pray, and reading Scriptures rightly. It's just ordinary stuff.

This promise of intimacy is both right and wrong. There is an intimacy with God, but it's like any other intimacy; it's part of the fabric of your life. In marriage you don't feel intimate most of the time. Nor with a friend. Intimacy isn't primarily a mystical emotion. It's a way of life, a life of openness, honesty, a certain transparency.

Doesn't the mystical tradition suggest otherwise?

One of my favorite stories is of Teresa of Avila. She's sitting in the kitchen with a roasted chicken. And she's got it with both hands, and she's gnawing on it, just devouring this chicken. One of the nuns comes in shocked that she's doing this, behaving this way. She said, "When I eat chicken, I eat chicken; when I pray, I pray."

If you read the saints, they're pretty ordinary people. There are moments of rapture and ecstasy, but once every ten years. And even then it's a surprise to them. They didn't do anything. We've got to disabuse people of these illusions of what the Christian life is. It's a wonderful life, but it's not wonderful in the way a lot of people want it to be.

Yet evangelicals rightly tell people they can have a "personal relationship with God." That suggests a certain type of spiritual intimacy.

All these words get so screwed up in our society. If intimacy means being open and honest and authentic, so I don't have veils, or I don't have to be defensive or in denial of who I am, that's wonderful. But in our culture, intimacy usually has sexual connotations, with some kind of completion. So I want intimacy because I want more out of life. Very seldom does it have the sense of sacrifice or giving or being vulnerable. Those are two different ways of being intimate. And in our American vocabulary *intimacy* usually has to do with getting something from the other. That just screws the whole thing up.

It's very dangerous to use the language of the culture to interpret the gospel. Our vocabulary has to be chastened and tested by revelation, by the Scriptures. We've got a pretty good vocabulary and syntax, and we'd better start paying attention to it because the way we grab words here and there to appeal to unbelievers is not very good.

This corruption of the word spirituality *even in Christian circles—does it have something to do with the New Age movement?*

The New Age stuff is old age. It's been around for a long time. It's a cheap shortcut to—I guess we have to use the word—*spirituality.* It avoids the ordinary, the everyday, the physical, the material. It's a form of Gnosticism, and it has a terrific appeal because it's a spirituality that doesn't have anything to do with doing the dishes or changing diapers or going to work. There's not much integration with work, people, sin, trouble, inconvenience.

I've been a pastor most of my life, for some forty-five years. I love doing this. But to tell you the truth, the people who give me the most distress are those who come asking, "Pastor, how can I be spiritual?" Forget about being spiritual. How about loving your husband? Now that's a good place to start. But that's not what they're interested in. How about learning to love your kids, accept them the way they are?

My name shouldn't even be connected with *spirituality.*

But it very much is.

I know. Then a few years ago I got this embarrassing position of being a professor of "spiritual theology" at Regent. Now what do you do?

You make spirituality sound so mundane.

I don't want to suggest that those of us who are following Jesus don't have any fun, that there's no joy, no exuberance, no ecstasy. They're just not what the consumer thinks they are. When we advertise the gospel in terms of the world's values, we lie to people. We lie to them, because this is a new life. It involves following Jesus. It involves the Cross. It involves death, an acceptable sacrifice. We give up our lives.

The Gospel of Mark is so graphic this way. The first half of the Gospel is Jesus showing people how to live. He's healing everybody. Then right in the middle, he shifts. He starts showing people how to die: "Now that you've got a life, I'm going to show you how to give it up." That's the whole spiritual life. It's learning how to die. And as you learn how to die, you start losing all your illusions, and you start being capable now to true intimacy and love.

It involves a kind of learned passivity, so that our primary mode of relationship is receiving, submitting, instead of giving and getting and doing. We don't do that very well. We're trained to be assertive, to get, to apply, or to consume and to perform.

Repentance, dying to self, submission—these are not very attractive hooks to draw people into the faith.

I think the minute you put the issue that way you're in trouble. Because then we join the consumer world, and everything then becomes product designed to give you something. We don't need something more. We don't need something better. We're after life. We're learning how to live.

I think people are fed up with consumer approaches, even though they're addicted to them. But if we cast the evangel in terms of benefits, we're setting people up for disappointment. We're telling them lies.

This is not the way our Scriptures are written. This is not the way Jesus came among us. It's not the way Paul preached. Where do we get all this stuff? We have a textbook. We have these Scriptures, and most of the time they're saying, "You're going the wrong way. Turn around. The culture is poisoning."

Do we realize how almost exactly the Baal culture of Canaan is reproduced in American church culture? Baal religion is about what makes you feel good. Baal worship is a total immersion in what I can get out of it. And of course, it was incredibly successful. The Baal priests could gather crowds that outnumbered followers of Yahweh twenty to one. There was sex, there was excitement, there was music, there was ecstasy, there was dance. "We got girls over here, friends. We got statues, girls, and festivals." This was great stuff. And what did the Hebrews have to offer in response? The Word. What's the Word? Well, Hebrews had festivals, at least!

Still, the one big hook or benefit to Christian faith is salvation, no? "Believe on the Lord Jesus Christ and you will be saved." Is this not something we can use to legitimately attract listeners?

It's the biggest word we have—*salvation,* being saved. We are saved from a way of life in which there was no resurrection. And we're being saved from ourselves. One way to define spiritual life is getting so tired and fed up with yourself you go on to something better, which is following Jesus.

But the minute we start advertising the faith in terms of benefits, we're just exacerbating the self problem. "With Christ, you're better, stronger, more likeable, you enjoy some ecstasy." But it's just more self. Instead, we want to get people bored with themselves so they can start looking at Jesus.

We've all met a certain type of spiritual person. She's a wonderful person. She loves the Lord. She prays and reads the Bible all the time. But all she thinks about is herself. She's not a selfish person. But she's always at the center of everything she's doing. "How can I witness better? How can I do this better? How can I take care of this person's problem better?" It's me, me, me disguised in a way that is difficult to see because her spiritual talk disarms us.

So how should we visualize the Christian life?

In church last Sunday, there was a couple in front of us with two bratty kids. Two pews behind us there was another couple with their two bratty kids making a lot of noise. This is mostly an older congregation. So these people are set in their ways. Their kids have been gone a long time. And so it wasn't a very nice service; it was just not very good worship. But afterwards I saw half a dozen of these elderly people come up and put their arms around the mother, touch the kids, sympathize with her. They could have been irritated.

Now why do people go to a church like that when they can go to a church that has a nursery, is air conditioned, and all the rest? Well, because they're Lutherans. They don't mind being miserable! Norwegian Lutherans!

And this same church recently welcomed a young woman with a baby and a three-year-old boy. The children were baptized a few weeks ago. But there was no man with her. She's never married; each of the kids has a different father. She shows up at church and wants her children baptized. She's a Christian and wants to follow in the Christian way. So a couple from the church acted as godparents. Now there are three or four couples in the church who every Sunday try to get together with her.

Now, where is the "joy" in that church? These are dour Norwegians! But there's a lot of joy. There's an abundant life going, but it's not abundant in the way a non-Christian would think. I think there's a lot more going on in churches like this; they're just totally anticultural. They're full of joy and faithfulness and obedience and care. But you sure wouldn't know it by reading the literature of church growth, would you?

*But many Christians would look at this church and say it's
dead, merely an institutional expression of the faith.*

What other church is there besides institutional? There's
nobody who doesn't have problems with the church,
because there's sin in the church. But there's no other
place to be a Christian except the church. There's sin
in the local bank. There's sin in the grocery stores. I
really don't understand this naïve criticism of the
institution. I really don't get it.

Frederick von Hugel said the institution of the
church is like the bark on the tree. There's no life in
the bark. It's dead wood. But it protects the life of the
tree within. And the tree grows and grows and grows
and grows. If you take the bark off, it's prone to disease, dehydration, death.

So, yes, the church is dead but it protects something alive. And when you try to have a church without bark, it doesn't last long. It disappears, gets sick,
and it's prone to all kinds of disease, heresy, and nar-
cissism.

In my writing, I hope to recover a sense of the
reality of congregation—what it is. It's a gift of the
Holy Spirit. Why are we always idealizing what
the Holy Spirit doesn't idealize? There's no idealiza-
tion of the church in the Bible—none. We've got two
thousand years of history now. Why are we so dumb?

*Since the Reformation, though, we've championed the idea
that the church can be reformed.*

Hasn't happened. I'm for always reforming, but to think
that we can get a church that's reformed is just silliness.

I think the besetting sin of pastors, maybe especially evangelical pastors, is impatience. We have a goal. We have a mission. We're going to save the world. We're going to evangelize everybody, and we're going to do all this good stuff and fill our churches. This is wonderful. All the goals are right. But this is slow, slow work, this soul work, this bringing people into a life of obedience and love and joy before God.

And we get impatient and start taking shortcuts and use any means available. We talk about benefits. We manipulate people. We bully them. We use language that is just incredibly impersonal—bullying language, manipulative language.

One doesn't normally think of churches as bullying.

Whenever guilt is used as a tool to get people to do anything—good, bad, indifferent—it's bullying. And then there's manipulative language—to talk people into programs, to get them involved, usually by promising them something.

I have a friend who is an expert at this sort of thing. He's always saying, "You've got to identify people's felt needs. Then you construct a program to meet the felt needs." It's pretty easy to manipulate people. We're so used to being manipulated by the image industry, the publicity industry, and the politicians that we hardly know we're being manipulated. This impatience to leave the methods of Jesus in order to get the work of Jesus done is what destroys spirituality, because we're using a nonbiblical, non-Jesus way to do what Jesus did. That's why spirituality is in such a mess as it is today.

But many pastors see people suffering in bad marriages,
with drug addiction, with greed. And so they
rightly want to help them now, by whatever method
will work.

Yes, except something backfires on you when you're
impatient. How do we meet the need? Do we do it in
Jesus' way or do we do it the Wal-Mart way?

Spirituality is not about ends or benefits or things;
it's about means. It's about *how* you do this. How do
you live in reality?

So, how do you help all these people? The needs
are huge. Well, you do it the way Jesus did it. You do
it one at a time. You can't do gospel work, kingdom
work in an impersonal way.

We live in the Trinity. Everything we do has to be
in the context of the Trinity, which means personally,
relationally. The minute you start doing things imper-
sonally, functionally, mass oriented, you deny the
gospel. Yet that's all we do.

Jesus is the Truth and the Life, but first he's the
Way. We can't do Jesus' work in the Devil's way.

I get exercised about this because many pastors
are getting castrated by these methodologies, which
are impersonal. There's no relationship to them. And
so they become performance oriented and successful.
It's pretty easy in our culture, at least if you're tall
and have a big smile. And they lose their soul. There's
nothing to them after twenty years. Or they crash.
They try all this stuff and it doesn't work, and they
quit, or quit and start doing something else. Probably
90 percent of the affairs that pastors have are not due
to lust, but boredom with not having this romantic
kind of life they thought they'd get.

*What if we were to frame this not in terms of needs but
    relevance? Many Christians hope to speak to genera-
    tion X or Y or postmoderns, or some subgroup, like
    cowboys or bikers—people for whom the typical
    church seems irrelevant.*

When you start tailoring the gospel to the culture,
    whether it's a youth culture, a generation culture, or
    any other kind of culture, you have taken the guts out
    of the gospel. The gospel of Jesus Christ is not the
    kingdom of this world. It's a different kingdom.
        My son Eric organized a new church six years
    ago. The Presbyterians have kind of a boot camp for
    new church pastors where you learn what you're
    supposed to do. So Eric went. One of the teachers
    there said he shouldn't put on a robe and a stole:
    "You get out there and you meet this generation
    where they are."
        So Eric, being a good student and wanting to
    please his peers, didn't wear a robe. His church
    started meeting in a high-school auditorium. He
    started out by wearing a business suit every Sunday.
    But when the first Sunday of Advent rolled around,
    and they were going to have Communion, he told
    me, "Dad, I just couldn't do it. So I put my robe on."
        Their neighbors, Joel and his wife, attended his
    church. Joel was the stereotype of the person the
    new church development was designed for—subur-
    ban, middle management, never been to church,
    totally secular. Eric figured he was coming because
    they were neighbors, or because he liked him. After
    that Advent service, he asked Joel what he thought of
    his wearing a robe.

He said, "It made an impression. My wife and I talked about it. I think what we're really looking for is sacred space. We both think we found it."

I think relevance is a crock. I don't think people care a whole lot about what kind of music you have or how you shape the service. They want a place where God is taken seriously, where they're taken seriously, where there is no manipulation of their emotions or their consumer needs.

Why did we get captured by this advertising, publicity mind-set? I think it's destroying our church.

But someone else might walk into Eric's church, see him with his robe, and walk out, thinking the whole place was too religious, too churchy.

So why are they going if it's not going to be religious? What do they go to church for?

Of course, there's another aspect to this. If you're going to a church where everybody's playing a religious role, that's going to be off-putting. But that performance mentality, role mentality can be seen in the cowboy church or whatever—everybody is performing a role there, too.

But we're involved with something that has a huge mystery to it. Are we going to wipe out all the mystery so we can be in control of it? Isn't reverence at the very heart of the worship of God?

And if we present a rendition of the faith in which all the mystery is removed, and there's no reverence, how are people ever going to know there's something more than just their own emotions, their own needs? There's something a lot bigger than my needs that's

going on. How do I ever get to that if the church service and worship program is all centered on my
needs?

Some people would argue that it's important to have a
worship service in which people feel comfortable so
they can hear the gospel.

I think they're wrong. Take the story I told you about this
family in front of us on Sunday. Nobody was comfortable. The whole church was miserable.
And yet, they might have experienced more gospel in
going up and putting their arms around that poor
mother, who was embarrassed to death.

How do we know when they have moved from merely
adapting ministry to the culture to sacrificing the
gospel?

One test I think is this: Am I working out of the Jesus
story, the Jesus methods, the Jesus way? Am I sacrificing relationship, personal attention, personal relationship for a shortcut, a program so I can get stuff
done? You can't do Jesus' work in a non-Jesus way
and get by with it—although you can be very "successful."
One thing that I think is characteristic of me is I
stay local. I'm rooted in a pastoral life, which is an
ordinary life. So while all this glitter and image of
spirituality is going around, I feel quite indifferent to
it, to tell you the truth. And I'm somewhat suspicious
of it because it seems to be uprooted, not grounded in
local conditions, which are the only conditions in
which you can live a Christian life.

ON REPRODUCTION AND THE IRREPRODUCIBLE GIFT
Christ, Conception, and Biotechnology
(From *The Cresset*)

Amy Laura Hall

She was only four months old. . . . Somewhat doubt-
fully her mother said we could hold her. . . . Since she
was not yet civilized, she made no insistent demands
on her momentary environment, but the process of
holding her was nevertheless vastly complicated. . . .
There were wriggling feet that had to be kept under a
blanket, a spine that needed support, and a head that
had to rest somewhere. . . . Clearly, the problem
called for a delicate fusion of mathematics and phys-
iology. . . . Of course, there was also an ethical problem. . . . She had little past and knew no future. . . .
For a moment everything in her life depended on the
efficiency with which we held her. . . .—if God continues to be patient, our momentary lovely burden
will hear the wild, mad, solemn bells ring on New
Year's Eve A.D. 2000. . . . Tonight her eyes are
unafraid and clear—staring into eyes that are fearful
of the anguished riddle of the years. . . . Sleep, my
baby, sleep—there are madmen across the two wide
waters who hold more of your temporal destiny in
their dripping hands than you know. . . . For a few
more years you will know only tenderness—until

one day you, too, will become aware of the world's seething cauldron of hate. . . . And then you, too, will begin to wonder—and you will do one of two things. . . . You will either putter around in life, content with building a wall and a web around your little plans and small hopes and creeping ambitions—or you will, if you believe in God (as I think you'd better) make your heart a chalice for a few drops of the world's blood and tears. . . . And when you know, finally, that the ultimate Good begins in Isaiah 53:6 and ends in John 3:16, you will be wise beyond man's knowing and strong beyond man's hope. . . .

Make your heart a chalice for a few drops of the world's blood and tears . . . and know finally that the ultimate Good begins in Isaiah 53:6 and ends in John 3:16. Or, alternatively, build a wall and a web around your little plans and small hopes and creeping ambitions. In these words from his column, "The Pilgrim," in the November 1937 issue of *The Cresset,* O. P. Kretzmann provokes the choice between these two paths; his words remain apt today.

Historian of Valparaiso University Richard Baepler writes of Dr. Kretzmann that he was "active in the Associated Lutheran Charities with its strong voice for social responsibility of the church particularly during the Depression." Dr. Kretzmann also "created and became editor of the first Lutheran journal aimed at commenting on cultural and political affairs from the stand-point of the Christian faith, called *The Cresset,* sponsored initially by the Walther League." Baepler adds, "Dr. Kretzmann was also a leader in the movement for liturgical reform, a movement to reemphasize the presence of the living Christ through the sacramental life of the church together—making Eucharist central and frequent and making baptism central for Lutheran churches."

These three commitments of O. P. Kretzmann—social responsibility, youth, and the sacramental life of the church tethered by Eucharist and Baptism—coincide, perhaps providentially, with our topic. How may we think about procreation—about conceiving life—if formed by the Christian liturgies of life? How may we think about procreation in the light of the new creation wrought by birth in Christ? How may we evaluate reproduction—reproducing life—when viewed through the irreproducible gift through whom we are made new?

The Problem

These questions preoccupy my work, and they have led me into the dusty archives of *Parents Magazine* and *Ladies' Home Journal,* to the proceedings of the Methodist Episcopal Church, and to a current Website for teenage mothers. I have slogged here to Valparaiso having been knee-deep in a research project to think theologically about biotechnology, and how biotechnology has shaped procreation and parenting in the United States. This work in archives and on the Internet and in the texts of Søren Kierkegaard, Karl Barth, and Helmut Thielicke is really neither fish nor fowl nor frog—in that I am not working in the field of bioethics as it is usually construed, nor cultural history as configured by secular historians, nor even theology as often described by professors of systematics. I have come to suspect that not one of those conversations alone, neither bioethics, nor history, nor even systematic theology—is sufficient to interrogate the present conundrums of scientifically enhanced procreation. Neither bioethics, nor cultural history, nor even perhaps traditional systematics may fully shock us awake and evoke the incarnate Hope sufficient to resist the allure of scientifically calibrated families, or the enhanced, supposedly perfected, child.

Stories of living people from parishes I have served and with whom I have worshipped echo in my mind as I work. An infertile couple going desperately into debt, spending tens of thousands of dollars to bear their own biologically related child. A single mother of two children diagnosed with ADHD who cannot afford to cut back on her work hours, and thus opting by what seems like necessity for the pharmaceutical solution to the chaos enveloping her family. A neighbor who confessed as we watched her five-year-old, curly-haired daughter canter in the grass that the little girl's twin sister had been selectively aborted, prenatally detected with Down Syndrome.

✴

Another story haunts me. A close family member is, like me, a minister. An early experience was serving in a smallish town relatively isolated from the big city, a town whose social life was still rooted in tangled memories of wealth newly acquired as well as wealth handed down. One morning a member of an old-moneyed family called to tell him that an eagerly anticipated grandchild had been born, the first child of a smart young professional and his bright-eyed wife. They did not want him to come to the hospital, however, because there was a problem. The baby girl had a cleft-palate. This pastor explained that, though he did not want to impose, he would like to come and be of whatever pastoral help he could. They reluctantly conceded. As he later related this story to me, his voice wavered as he explained that the mother had held her daughter close, wrapped up in the little pink hospital blankets. She did not want him to see the child's face. Perhaps due to the pastor's patience, perhaps due to grace, the mother eventually unwrapped her child and showed her to the pastor. He could find no words other than "She's beautiful." She was, he explained, beautiful.

They waited until the baby had gone through the corrective surgery to have her baptized. This was perhaps what troubled this pastor most. He encouraged them to bring her to church, to allow the congregation to embrace her and them and to receive the child into the community of faith through the re-creation of baptism. But they kept her hidden until after the surgery. He said that the family seemed not only scared but also, in a way that he could not immediately interpret, ashamed. Perhaps, he thought, this had to do somehow with the association of cleft-palate and being lower-class—a loose association, due to the fact that only more wealthy families could afford this surgery in decades past.

This story of understandable fear and delayed baptism serves as a focal point for me. How might a focus on the extravagant, re-creating Gift of Christ allow Christians to view this child, this beautiful and unexpected girl, as a gift? Are Christians able to see even disability as part of the gift of new life in baptism? How did some Christians in the United States come to see some children as accidental, as mistakes, as sources of shame?

In Karl Barth's *Church Dogmatics,* there is a short passage that can, I believe, go some way toward interpreting this story, as well as many of the images of anxious, class-conscious procreation I dig up in my archival work.

On the contrary, it is one of the consolations of the coming kingdom and expiring time that this anxiety about posterity, that the burden of the postulate that we should and must bear children, heirs of our blood and name and honour and wealth, that the pressure and bitterness and tension of this question, if not the question itself, is removed from us all by the fact that *the Son on whose birth alone everything seriously and ultimately depended has now become our Brother.* No one now has to be conceived and born. We need not expect any other than the One of whose coming we are certain because He is already come. [emphasis added]

There are many ways to sort through the biotechnological revolution in procreation and parenting—some consider the normativity of nature, thinking with natural law illumined by Revelation on the ways that we are created to bear and care for children. It is also potentially fruitful to think about biotechnology in light of grace, in light of the one irreproducible gift Who may shape the gift of reproduction. No one particularly preconceived, hoped-for child must now be born, because the one promised child, foretold long ago, has been born. The command to be fruitful, to multiply strong and reliable children capable of carrying the promise, is now set within a context, is now relative to the particular fruit of a holy womb. With the birth of this promised one, the pressure and bitterness and tension of conceiving and crafting heirs of blood and name and honor and wealth are removed. Perhaps the form of parenting itself should be shaped by the form of the one born to empty himself for our sakes. If, to quote Pastor Kretzmann, "the ultimate Good begins in Isaiah 53:6 and ends in John 3:16," should not the good of procreation, of bearing and caring for children, be shaped by that Good? Should not Christian parenting bear the marks, so to speak, of this same Good?

In mainline Protestantism in the United States, the biotechnological practices of parenting have not been so clearly marked by grace. Purveyors of anxious reproduction have found ready Christian participants down through the centuries A.D. Premonitory parenting is not a unique invention of the biotechnological West. All languages intersect at the expectant or barren womb, and each generation of Christians faces a constellation of temptations that may shape the task of conceiving and raising children. The desire to craft and manipulate conception in order to graft power to power, and so to cultivate wealth, was at one time the domain of royalty and their eager courtiers. Those who fell drastically below such aspirations sought mere survival. But in the last one hundred or so years, Christians in North America (more than elsewhere) have seen a simultaneous democratization and a technical manipulation of aspiring parenthood that reflects a parental desire to thrive and flourish through promised and promising children.

The American dream of remaking each generation according to human ingenuity is as old as Benjamin Franklin. Who can argue against bearing and raising promising children? But Christians must ask, "Which promise?" By which promise are Christians presently shaping our children? I watch the children of privilege at Duke negotiate daily the route to a promise of wealth, success, independence, and I wonder. . . . How does the coming of the true Promised One align our own hopes for promising families? Are Christian parents content with building a wall around our neighborhoods and our homes, weaving a web around little plans and small hopes and creeping ambitions? Or, are Christian families making their homes a chalice for a few drops of the world's blood and tears?

Suspicions

For many mainline Protestants, the answer to this question appears to be the former rather than the latter choice. What began for me as a project morally to evaluate specific procedures and techniques in contemporary reproductive and pediatric medicine has become a larger inquiry into the particularly mainline Protestant flavor of biotechnological reproduction in the United States. Digging through magazines and tracts, I routinely came across the image of the well-managed, orderly, nuclear Protestant family. As it turns out, mainline Protestants—my people—have had a particular role in the growth of commercialized medicine. While more fundamentalist Protestants and Roman Catholics by and large resisted various products and practices in the medicalization of parenting, mainline Protestants duly applied their famous work ethic to the prevailing spirit of reproduction and child care, making diligent use of the tools widely available through medical science in order to craft children that would measure up and families that would fit in.

To some extent, the question of family planning, of using the proper, new tools to time procreation, is an underlying difference between Roman Catholics and Protestants in the United States, but the ways that mainline Protestants, at least, legitimized the tools of timing reflected assumptions about the "good of families" and the "promise" being sought. By way of "modern" infant formula, atomic science, tomes of expert advice, and the careful breeding of "fitter families," middle-class Protestants industriously sought to differentiate their own families from families that were "unplanned," "accidental," and "irresponsible." As I went digging, I began more and more to suspect that there was something amiss here in the pursuit of responsible normalcy, even while that pursuit might look formally similar to the pursuit of a godly, ordered life.

First, this pursuit of normalcy traded on the "other" family by which "good" parents could be distinguished. I suspect that good middle-class families needed the "questionable" families in order to prove their own legitimacy. I am not sure yet whether to call this role of the "bad" families and "bad" children a need or a fear. Perhaps it is somehow both. The marketing of many of the relevant technologies and "expert advice" seems to have both created and tapped into the fear that parents had regarding unsavory, suboptimal children and families.

United Methodist grandmothers in my hometown subtly click their tongues and shake their heads when they see a baby without shoes. Socks do not count. My usual tactic with this generation of women, to explain to them that pediatricians now advise against X, Y, or Z, does not work regarding shoes. By the code of aspiring women in West Texas, newfangled podiatrists are less trustworthy than the echoes of old wisdom. "Trashy children" go barefoot. Good mothers put shoes on their babies. Passed down from depression-era great-grandmothers, the now-ghostly presence of Appalachian boys and girls, bellies distended from hookworm, still haunts the Sears and Roebucks in San Angelo, Texas. Two retired schoolteachers thus exchange knowing looks as an unshod toddler is wheeled by in an umbrella stroller. By way of such sense, families with Merle Haggard roots elbow and nudge their way up toward Pat Boone.

Isn't this climb, by way of defining one's own children as children of "distinction," contrary to the form of life shaped by the Gift of Christ? The coming of the one, irreproducible gift is a thoroughly soteriological event, but it is also an event that can pattern one's life to receive the gift of children without the anxious need to justify them. We mainline Protestants, eager to fit within the bounds of "Good Housekeeping" culture, have aligned ourselves with those who similarly fit. The freedom born of being reborn in Christ may instead allow parents to risk not only association with but real proximity to the very families, children, and neighborhoods "good housekeeping" disposes us to avoid.

Another related suspicion is that aspiring families have legitimized, and then had to try to keep up with, a culture that is deeply inhospitable to incarnate, dependent life. The modern, medically calibrated family is thus not only ungracious but also impossibly inhospitable. Most often in the last century, the "other" family has been the "profligate," "inefficient," overly and overtly dependent family. The family that can function seamlessly in the present economy is, more or less, labeled "good." As respectable parenthood grew in the last century to become synonymous with the efficient flow of home economics and civil economies, many middle-class families sought to cushion themselves from all avoidable forms of suffering and physical need. As a certain class of children became technological products for manipulation, society became ever less capable of adapting to the pace of relatively inefficient time required by all children. Current patterns of biotechnological reproduction and child care are problematic in ways that reflect this history; not only do such patterns dehumanize capable children as projects for technological manipulation, they also serve to diagnose overtly dependent children—whether disabled or poor— as woefully unplanned.

Forming a More Perfect Union

The most blatant example in recent history of the union of Protestant class politics and reproductive science occurred during the rise of eugenics in the first half of the twentieth century. Although a growing number of people are aware of the patently coercive antimiscegenation and sterilization laws associated with the eugenics movement in the United States, fewer know about the simultaneous effort to shape the imaginations of middle-class Christians toward "voluntary" eugenics. This "Fitter Family" movement, which flourished in the United States from the turn of the last century until World War II, was engineered by the American Eugenics Society and sought to encourage "prudent" marriages and to discourage the unfit or "tainted" from procreating. Bringing the "science" of eugenics into American churches, homes, and county fairs, exhibits across the heartland warned white Americans, "Some are born to be a burden on the rest" and explicitly linked crime and unemployment to ill-considered conception. While the vast majority of Roman Catholic and fundamentalist Christians refused these efforts, many mainline Protestant leaders took up the charge with gusto, preaching sermons and crafting Sunday School curricula consistent with the plan. In the resulting rhetoric, middle-class Protestants sought to separate themselves from dissolutely reproducing immigrants, "irresponsible" African Americans, and the deviant, accidental children of lower-class Anglos. The specters of the diseased or disabled child and that of the overwhelming poor became intertwined in the middle-class imagination. Eager to contribute to, rather than cause a drain on, the variously precarious economy of early twentieth-century America, many mainline Protestant leaders became advocates of a responsibly planned parenthood.

What about less mainline, mainstream Protestants? What about conservative, white evangelicals in the United States? Christine Rosen has written a groundbreaking and, for some, a counterintuitive new book on religion and eugenics in twentieth-century America. In her *Preaching Eugenics: Religious Leaders and the American Eugenics Movement,* she concludes her research thus:

> Religious leaders pursued eugenics precisely when they moved away from traditional religious tenets. The liberals and modernists in their respective faiths—those who challenged their churches to conform to modern circumstances—became the eugenics movement's most enthusiastic supporters.

According to Rosen's research, it was those religious leaders who overestimated the mastery of the biological sciences and underestimated the gratuity of God's creation who were most susceptible to the summons to craft particular kinds of scientifically enhanced families. More often than not, more conservative, scripturally based Christians in America were suspicious of the claim, made monthly in early issues of *Parents Magazine,* that "The Nation Marches Forward on the Feet of Little Children."

This brings us back to O. P. Kretzmann's circle of influence, and to one of his colleagues, Walter A. Maier. Dennis Durst writes of Maier, a pastor who served for many years as editor of the youth-oriented *Walther League Messenger* and who became the leading voice of the immensely popular radio ministry, "The Lutheran Hour":

The crux of [Maier's] critique was thus, "Ultimately, eugenics leaves no room for God. If we cannot run the world of today without God, how can we hope to govern the generation of tomorrow without divine sanction and supervision?" ... Maier attacked eugenics as an egregious instance of pride. ... For Maier, the eugenics movement, which he derided as "this cult of the superman," was guilty of promoting social injustice. He found the studies on tenement dwellers by eugenicists as both condescending and "a startling contradiction of Christian ideals." Couching his criticism in terms evocative of an ethos both biblical and democratic, Maier asserted, "To prevent underprivileged individuals from accepting their inalienable and divinely bestowed pleasures of parenthood is not only a physiological error, but it is also an act of presumptuous discrimination."

While Maier was not an unambiguous character, Lutherans may be properly inspired by the role he played alongside other conservative Protestants when so many other Christians in the United States were jumping on the eugenics bandwagon. While Harry Emerson Fosdick and many other "progressive" mainline Protestants were preaching eugenics from their pulpits, Maier saw that there was something unfaithful, prideful, and ungracious about determining who is and is not fit to enter into the difficult but joyful work of bearing children.

How might we Christians of today determine our role in the midst of the pressure to perform and craft families of distinction and safety? How are we to counter the almost overwhelming messages in popular magazines and on the *Lifetime* channel, messages of anxious, walled-up, and webbed-around little hopes and dreams? Allow me to make this even more real. If we are bound for the promised land of middle- or upper-middle-class parenting in the United States, how are we to resist the allure of the promising family? How are we to resist the call to buy a house in the best neighborhood, take the best pharmaceuticals, get all of the prenatal tests, and procure, if necessary, the best termination in order to produce a child of real promise?

Charity

One way to resist the allure is to find stories of resistance, and to recall them daily. There was recently a young woman at the Kennedy School of Government who took in foster babies. Single, twenty-seven years old, and a student, this woman cared for newborns while they went through the detox process and/or waited for the paperwork for adoption by other waiting parents. The pictures of her on the Harvard Website feature her in the library with a newborn in a carrier strapped to her chest. When I first heard about this young woman, I was eager to know more about her. How did she decide to do this? Why in the world would she take this on while a student at one of the most challenging professional schools in the nation? The way to advance at such an institution is to appear as unencumbered, as independent, as shorn of as much embodied responsibility as is possible. How did this young woman summon up the courage to link her life up with children who so clearly embody need and dependence?

As she put it, she just wanted to do a bit of something good. Noting, while a volunteer in a neonatal unit, that there were infants who received no visitors, she decided to try to be of use. When someone asked her whether she has a difficult time letting go when it is time for the infants to leave her, she replied, "they deserve someone to cry for them." Her name, believe it or not, is Charity Bell. Perhaps her mother had this in mind for her all along. I suspect that our Heavenly Father has this sort of thing in mind for many of us.

There is a trajectory of Lutheran thought running through Kierkegaard, Thielicke, and (most clearly, the early) Barth, that narrates discipleship as patterned by openness to the interruption of Christ into the world. While each of these theologians sounds a counter-note of responsibility, such responsibility is embedded in the larger context of receptivity to the unlikely and irreproducible gift of grace. By way of this strand in the Protestant tradition, the command to multiply is properly seen within the revelation that life itself is a loan, a gift that never truly becomes ours for disposal, justification, manipulation, or definitive control. To envision the gift of reproduction and parenting as set within the narrative of the irreproducible Gift that is Christ should, as Barth describes above, shift the task away from our mastery of the future. The gift of Christ in Baptism and Eucharist may open our domestic lives up to be a chalice for a few drops of the world's blood and tears.

❧

During a speaking engagement, someone from the audience asked me "What are children for?" As I struggled to answer, a Mennonite answered, "Well, our children are born to be martyrs." While I cannot go there with my Mennonite brother, I believe that justification by faith may infuse the order of creation known as the Christian family with a willingness to take real risks for the sake of the Gospel. We may risk the shame of a teenage pregnancy, if the alternative is abortion. We may risk adopting children who are themselves "at risk," allowing our lives to become thereby less secure. We may even have the courage to bind our lives with foster children, allowing them to interrupt our lives and receive our love even knowing they will leave us soon.

The child who occasions the kingdom has already come, has been born in an inauspicious manger, has lived with offensive openness to the wounds of the poor and the just plain sinful, and has died a criminal's death so that our lives might be made holy. To raise children in the wake of that life and in the growing tide of that kingdom is a project that will likely make Christians seem irresponsible and even profligate to a culture intent on raising heirs of honor and wealth. I pray that our faith may lead us to refuse the messages of pressurized, taut parenting, eschewing the tools of medicalized class warfare in order to live instead at the untidy intersection of real bodies, real wounds, and real need.

ODD JOB

(From *The Christian Century*)

Richard Lischer

According to new findings in the Pulpit & Pew National Clergy Survey, a solid majority of clergy is deeply satisfied with the pastoral ministry. Seven out of ten of those surveyed report they have never considered abandoning their vocation. In other words, most pastors claim to have found happiness in the ministry.

Why is this disturbing? Some of us in academia have made a decent living chronicling the malaise of our fellow clergy. For years we've had our students read the appropriate literature—from *Elmer Gantry* to *Wise Blood*—on the implicit assumption that these and other portraits of slightly out-of-whack ministers accurately represent the norm of vocational misery among Protestant clergy. Indeed, the tormented Hazel Motes in Flannery O'Connor's *Wise Blood* appears to have more in common with the tormented apostle Paul than those, like us, who have found happiness in ministry.

In 2 Corinthians, Paul narrates his ministry as a continuous near-death experience, as if ministry consists of thousands of mini-funerals and mini-Easters—moments of truth when this heartbreak or that betrayal, this breakthrough or that triumph puts the crucified and risen Lord right there with him on the razor's edge of ministry.

"For while we live, we are always being given up to death for Jesus' sake, so that the life of Jesus may be manifested in our mortal flesh [the flesh of ministry]. So death is at work in us, but life in you." Later, in a typical 110-word sentence, Paul pushes the envelope of language as he throws out image after ecstatic image of hard times on the mission circuit—of calamities, beatings and imprisonments, of being treated "as unknown and yet are well known"—when he blurts out, "As dying—and look!—we live."

This is all very dramatic, but many ministers are weary with the overwork and emotional fatigue of the office. They have significant reservations about this cruciform metaphor for ministry. Paul's theology appears to provide a rationale for the victimization of the clergy, what Joseph Sittler called the maceration of the minister.

And yet, what Paul really offers is an escape from the macerating criteria for evaluating the effectiveness of a ministry. He offers a conception of ministry that focuses on the work itself and not on the conditions or the outcomes of the work. His dialectic of death and resurrection suggests a realism that transcends our language of happiness and unhappiness in ministry. Indeed, it forges a tool for critiquing our best notions of happy and unhappy, satisfied and dissatisfied, successful and unsuccessful.

"Having this ministry," he says, "by the mercy of God, we do not lose heart." The phrase reminds us that this thing we are accustomed to acquire, analyze, and discuss at conferences is a blazing fire that cannot be touched. It is holy. It is a gift, as Paul says in Ephesians, a grace "given to me for you."

The question is, what kind of gift is ministry? It is the kind of gift that requires hours and hours of assembly, the sort of gift that you know, even as you take it out of the box, you will one day be very sorry to have received. You know exactly what kind of gift is coming when the giver says, "Here, this gift is for you. Try not to let it discourage you."

"Oh, all this heartache for little me—you really shouldn't have." It's as if Paul understands that our truest heartaches, like his, derive not from the culture, the economy, or the political climate, but from the ministry. The heartaches are not cured by ministry, they are caused by ministry. Having this ministry is like having children. Yes, in some respects they are an answer to prayer, but they also stimulate a lot of desperate prayers. And all the joy they bring into your life is sharpened by the possibilities of new pain.

✶

One Sunday in our congregation we baptized a baby the day after its mother's funeral. It fell to our minister to "make sense" of these two events in words. I can still see him pacing up and down the center aisle with the baby in the crook of his arm. Through his tears he spoke of the promises of God, as if to say, "This is the ministry we have. It's a hard gift. Let's not lose heart."

This ministry is like love: it never ends. It never comes to the end of its rope. It never wrings its hands and says, "There's nothing more to be done." By its very nature it can never run out of material, because the very conditions of its defeat only create the possibilities for its rebirth.

Can a war defeat ministry? No. War produces an occasion for the ministry of comfort and justice. Can conflicts over sexuality destroy ministry? We are tempted to say yes, but even Paul would say they elicit the ministry of reconciliation. Can death bring ministry to an end? No, as one of Georges Bernanos's characters in *The Diary of a Country Priest* says to the new pastor. "Love is stronger than death—that stands within your books."

There is something about this ministry that cannot be captured even by professionals, which is why, I suspect, Paul refers to it elsewhere as a "secret." I rejoice with the seven in ten who will not renounce their vocation. I rejoice with any who are foolish enough to admit they are satisfied, even happy, in ministry, because they are obviously in on the secret. They must be. If you live in a world like ours whose attitude toward ministry runs the gamut from condescension to contempt, you would have to be crazy to say, "I love the ministry!"—unless, of course, you are in on the secret and have what Paul had. Unless you have glimpsed its holiness and apprehended it for the gift that it is. Unless you too have experienced its hard-won joy.

ISLAMIC COUNTER-REFORMATION

(From *First Things*)

Paul Marshall

Here in the West, one response to the growth of militant extremist Islam has been to suggest that Islam needs a "reformation"—that is, some kind of reform and renewal. I do not want to read too much into this rather loose application of the term, but I think it can be misleading if it suggests that the need is for an Islamic renewal broadly analogous to the sixteenth-century Protestant efforts to renew the Catholic Church. My own view is that many of the problems of contemporary Islam are more like Protestant problems than like Catholic problems, and therefore that something more akin to a dilution of Protestantism is required. Perhaps instead we should be urging an Islamic "Counter-Reformation."

Let's begin with Scripture. One Protestant emphasis is *sola scriptura,* which stresses reliance on the Bible alone, rather than on tradition, reason, and natural law thinking. Might there be a parallel in Islam, where one of the problems in contemporary thought, especially amongst more reactionary thinkers, is precisely scripturalism and literalism? Wahhabis, for example, seem to believe that they can start the process of interpretation of the Koran and the *hadith* anew, without reliance on traditional Islamic schools of law, theology, and philosophy. Hence they move in a mechanical way from the ancient text to its present application in sheer disregard of the myriad hermeneutical problems over which they glide.

This has few, if any, parallels in the contemporary Christian world (the widespread use of the pop sociological term "fundamentalist" notwithstanding). Since the Bible is acknowledged by even the most conservative to have been composed by many authors, in many genres and styles, over many centuries, in several languages, Christianity and Judaism have developed modes of exegesis in which very different styles of literature need to be reconciled into a more or less coherent whole. Even the most conservative Baptist does not take literally the prophecies in Daniel or the images in the Book of Revelation. Across the board they are seen as highly figurative texts, certainly not to be taken as realist descriptions. Indeed, the current American spate of interest in apocalyptic prophecy stems precisely from attempts to draw meaning from complex and difficult imagery.

By contrast, the Koran is understood by Muslims to have been revealed directly to Mohammed over a few short years—while the *hadith* cover only what Mohammed said and did—and the language and style are relatively consistent. All of this makes the development of any literary interpretive tradition in Islam very unlikely; to encourage even greater reliance on a *sola scriptura* approach would only compound the problem of literalistic scripturalism.

The other side of this stress on Scripture is a comparative neglect of reason and natural law. This point can be overstressed, since no significant Protestant rejected either (though Luther in his bad moods came close), but it is fair to say that these have been less than central in Protestantism. There seems to have been a similar pattern in recent Islam, wherein scripturalism and literalism have displaced philosophical and theological reflection.

It was not always this way. The Mu'tazilites, who sought to enrich their religious reflection through the study of Greek philosophy, were a dominant force in the ninth-century Abbasid Caliphate. Sufis do similar things with mystic and spiritual thought. These movements have always existed in Islam. But the current wave of radical Islam, which is what prompts our calls for reformation, has downplayed or rejected these currents, and often persecuted their proponents.

The weakness of such reflection in contemporary Islam makes it harder for Muslims to debate, agree, or disagree either with one another or with non-Muslims, and vice versa. As John Courtney Murray observed, even disagreement is a genuine achievement: it requires that we first engage with and understand each other. In the modern age, we often never get as far as disagreeing: instead we assume that our opponents are irrational or wicked and so simply talk past them or denounce them.

This absence of general agreement or disagreement reveals how weak is much of our current intellectual engagement with Islam. A thousand years ago the greatest minds of Christianity, Judaism, and Islam—such as Thomas Aquinas, Maimonides, Al-Farabi, and Averroes—were engaged in fundamental debate about the nature of revelation, faith, reason, law, and political authority. In their disagreements they created a common discourse across their religious boundaries. In the modern age we are left instead with vacuous, and therefore futile, calls for toleration and diversity.

A similar problem occurs with discussions of natural law. If one believes that there is a natural law and that this law springs from God (as an expression of God's reason), Scripture can be understood also as teaching that law, and the law can be seen, at least in some cases, as lying within the text. This allows us to study Scripture in such a way as to discern an underlying body of systematic thought. Hence, for example, the requirement of Islamic law (*sharia*) to have four witnesses in order to secure a conviction for certain types of crime can be understood as a demand to make very sure that there is adequate evidence for such a conviction. In a desert society, of course, witnesses may be the only form of proof, and so their testimony is required. In a modern society, however, such evidence as fingerprinting, DNA testing, or other forensic means could be understood as fulfilling the same goal and thus meeting the standard required by the text. The text, then, is understood not as primarily about numbers of witnesses but as a call for legal reliability and consistency in the rules of evidence.

A contrary view, a type of nominalism associated at its inception with William of Occam, would be that law, and thus good and evil, are rooted simply in God's will, with no necessary rational structure. Their reality is to be accepted rather than understood. This approach seems to be common in certain Islamic circles, which maintain that the text simply says what it says, with nothing beneath the surface, and so we must simply repeat it to the letter.

Connected to this stress on Scripture and relative downplaying of tradition, philosophy, and natural law is decentralization and fragmentation. Following the Protestant Reformation there began a proliferation of denominations and churches, a process that has continued into the twenty-first century and has now produced many independent congregations and clergy. In the United States, independent pastors and preachers can start churches or run newspapers, magazines, publishing houses, colleges, seminaries, radio stations, and TV stations. Since in practice their authority stems from their charisma (in the Weberian, if not necessarily the Pentecostal, sense), these pastors often have more power than their nominal governing boards and are subject to little structured accountability so long as they are successful. In the absence of a magisterium, the question of authority lies open, and such independent operators can maintain authority within their organizations so long as they continue to attract a following.

In Sunni Islam a similar fragmentation has occurred. Despite the authority of institutions such as Al-Azhar University in Egypt, and despite the high regard given to learning, a teacher or jurist can gain authority if he can draw followers. In practice such leaders can establish their own mosques and madrassas, as well as radio and TV shows. Osama bin Laden, it should be remembered, is an engineer, not a jurist, but in practice he can issue *fatwas* that have tremendous influence.

I am not suggesting that extremist Islam and terrorism find a counterpart in some conservative branches of Protestantism. Despite the fevered imaginings of some secularists who try to include them both as subspecies of a dubious general category of religious extremism, they are very different. Nevertheless some parallels between Protestant Christianity and contemporary Islam are worth considering. Both can tend to scripturalism, a relative downgrading of reason and natural law, fragmentation, and a proliferation of authority centers. In this situation, it might be good to put aside calls that suggest analogies to the Reformation and instead think about whether Islam might be helped by something akin to a "Catholicization." I have no idea whether this is possible, but I do suggest that it might be a more useful metaphor for renewal in Islam.

It also suggests that we must think more deeply than most of us have about the actual intellectual content of Islamic terrorism. Much of our discourse implies that such extremists are people without ideas or rationale. We often simply call them "terrorists," but of course that tells us almost nothing. As Daniel Pipes has pointed out, terrorism is merely a means to an end: it is neither an end nor a rationale for an end. There are many different types of terrorists in the world. The Tamil Tigers in Sri Lanka, for example, have long engaged in terrorist suicide bombings, but while we may oppose them, they are not those with whom we are currently engaged in war.

At other times, extremist Muslims are simply described as hate-filled and evil. Such pejoratives also tell us very little about who they are, what they think, and what they want. After all, the world is replete with hate-filled and evil people, but most of them are not terrorists.

Alternatively, they are referred to by that old standby, "fundamentalist," a word dredged from the American past and of dubious provenance and meaning even there. Despite the efforts of sociologists and psychologists to give it some determinate content, it has never really transcended the common connotation of "religious nutcase"—or, perhaps more accurately, "religious nutcase with whom I disagree." Use of this word generally indicates a disposition to treat an ideological movement as if it were a personality type; it usually signifies a refusal to take seriously what people say they actually believe. "Fundamentalists" are people to be diagnosed rather than heard.

In any case, the term has little relation to terrorism or to the type of extremism with which we are concerned. Perhaps the most "fundamentalist" Christian groups in the United States are the Amish, the Hutterites, and the old-order Mennonites—but few people lie awake at night for fear of Amish terrorism.

Psychologising can be a way of evading any real effort to understand religious beliefs. Another evasive tactic is to treat such professed beliefs merely as the sublimation of drives that can be explained by poverty, economic change, or the stresses of modernity. Of course, these factors may play a role: no part of human life is sealed off from any other. But instead of an effort at understanding, too often what we see is a methodological commitment to treat religion as secondary, as an evanescent and derivative phenomenon that may be explained away but can never be used to explain. In the face of extremist Islam, this kind of mindlessness is intellectual suicide.

Genuine mindfulness about the beliefs and aspirations of Islam is demonstrated for us by such thinkers as Bernard Lewis, who traces the precipitous decline of the Islamic world in the last five centuries and shows how much of the Muslim community asks itself continually the question "What went wrong?" Islamism and terrorism provide the latest of a series of answers to that galling question. Their answer is that Muslims have forsaken the purity of early Islam and have gone whoring after foreign, especially Western, ways. Their solution is an Islamic revival that will institute reactionary Islamic law throughout the world and restore the lost Caliphate; moreover, violence can and must be used to expel the West (understood as Christendom) and coerce fellow Muslims into the right path.

Bin Laden in his 1998 interview on Al-Jazeera television declared, "There are two parties to the conflict: world Christianity, which is allied with Jews and Zionism, led by the United States, Britain, and Israel. The second party is the Islamic world." His 1998 merger with Egypt's Islamic Jihad formed the World Islamic Front for Holy War Against Jews and Crusaders, and he has described President Bush as fighting under the "sign of the cross." Al-Qaeda's manual begins by recalling "the fall of our orthodox Caliphates on March 3, 1924." Bin Laden's November 3, 2001, videotape proclaims, "Following World War I, which ended more than eighty-three years ago, the whole Islamic world fell under the Crusader banner." The grievance, continually expressed, is the collapse of the Islamic Caliphate and the Islamic world generally in the face of Christendom.

Islamist terrorism is not simply rooted in ignorance or poverty or in reactions to American policy in the Middle East. It is rooted in a religiously informed view of the world. To fight extremist Islam without engaging these religious ideas would be akin to fighting communism without bothering to learn anything of Marxism or Leninism.

An Islamic Counter-Reformation would require many things. One is a reconsideration of the work of the Mu'-tazilites. This would mean reopening the gate of *ijtihad* (interpretation), which has been closed in Sunni Islam for many centuries. Along with such a revival of *ijtihad* would have to come theological reflection on the relation between revelation and history, along with the hermeneutical questions and opportunities that such reflection would bring with it. Many Muslims view the effects of biblical criticism in the West with skepticism and believe that it has been a major factor in undermining the strength of Christianity. There is truth in this, but it is not the only possible outcome: there are modes of biblical and historical criticism now accepted by nearly all Christians, including the most orthodox.

When it comes to sources of authority, it is doubtful that Islam ever will, or ever should, have a formal magisterium. Al-Azhar has never been able to fill that role. But it may be possible and good to have a quasi-magisterium. This would require developing networks of moderate Islamic scholars and lawyers who could formulate joint *fatwas* in opposition to those issued by radicals, who are currently much better funded and organized. Such projects are currently under way, but they are still in their infancy.

Whether there will be a Counter-Reformation in Islam is, of course, something that Muslims will have to decide for themselves. But non-Muslims can help to encourage it, not least by engaging with Islam in a way that does not flinch from criticizing the religion, even while recognizing its considerable dignity and worth. Taking Islam seriously demands nothing less.

THE MEANING OF
CHRIST'S SUFFERING

(From *Books & Culture*)

Frederica Mathewes-Green

Most movies wait till after they're released to stir up controversy, but Mel Gibson's *The Passion of the Christ* has been preceded by nearly a year of fisticuffs. It provided an unusually rich opportunity for people who don't know what they're talking about to do just that. I'll continue that tradition by admitting that, as I write this, I still have not seen the film. I expect it will be good moviemaking, a powerful example of the artistic possibilities of film. I hope it will stir up old faith in Christians and break forth new faith in unbelievers.

But as I read interviews with Gibson before the release, one theme caught my attention. Listen to this quote, for example. In the September 15, 2003, *New Yorker,* Gibson told Peter J. Boyer, "I wanted to bring you there. I wanted to be true to the Gospels. That has never been done before."

That goal meant showing us what real scourging and crucifixion would look like. "I didn't want to see Jesus looking really pretty," Gibson went on. "I wanted to mess up one of his eyes, destroy it."

Now, if you're like me, you registered a double take. Surely, the Crucifixion and its preceding torture were brutal events. But there's nothing in the Gospels specifically about Jesus' eye being destroyed. Didn't Gibson say he wanted to make this movie absolutely true to the Gospels, as "has never been done before"?

So I tried to picture a movie that reflected only what the Gospels tell us, and realized that there's not much there about the gore. A lot of each Gospel concerns the Passion, of course; nineteenth-century theologian Martin Kahler said that the Gospels are "passion narratives with extended introductions." Yet those narratives mostly record the swirl of events around Jesus in his last days, what people said and did. The description of his physical sufferings is as minimal as the writers can make it.

"Having scourged Jesus, Pilate delivered him to be crucified," the Synoptic Gospels (Matthew, Mark, Luke) agree. "When they came to the place which is called The Skull, there they crucified him." Little more than a dozen verses later he is dead.

I'm not questioning whether the Passion actually was brutal. And I'm not questioning whether an artist is free to depict it however he likes. The thing I'm curious about is: why did Christians in the first millennium choose to depict it differently?

Did they avoid the bloody details because they were squeamish? Not St. Luke, who, though one of the most elegant New Testament writers, describes Judas' death in more graphic detail than we asked for: "Falling headlong he burst open in the middle and all his bowels gushed out" (Acts 1:18).

Were they ashamed of the Cross, an emblem of criminal execution? Not St. Paul, who states: "Far be it from me to glory except in the Cross of our Lord Jesus Christ" (Galatians 6:14).

Were the brutal elements of a crucifixion so familiar that they needed no elaboration? Yet the pain that Christ endured was exactly what later Christians cherished; if the early church had felt the same way, mere familiarity would not have quenched devotion. A lover does not grow weary of contemplating his beloved's face. But rather than poring over the details of Christ's suffering, earlier Christians averted their eyes.

Graphic meditation on Christ's suffering doesn't appear before the late medieval era, approximately the fourteenth century. Before that, the presentation is more in accord with the way Christ appears in the Gospel of John. In iconography, he reigns serene from the Cross, a victorious conqueror who has rescued us from Death.

In fact, the concept of "rescue" is the key. The wounds that Christ sustained are like those of a hero. Imagine that a young policeman has rescued some hostages at great physical cost, including his own capture and torture. It would be unseemly, even insulting, to continually ask him, "How did it feel when they tortured you? What did it look like? Where did you bleed?" The officer would understandably wish you'd focus not on his humiliation but on his victory.

That's the attitude we see in ancient hymns from Holy Week:

> The sun was darkened, for it could not bear to see such outrage done to God, before whom all things tremble.... When Thou was crucified, O Christ, all the creation saw and trembled. The foundations of the earth quaked in fear of thy power. The lights of heaven hid themselves.... The hosts of angels were amazed.

A hymn from the fourth-century Liturgy of St. Basil is familiar even to some Protestants: "Let all earthly flesh keep silent, and with fear and trembling stand."

Devotion didn't simply change with the times; the same awe-filled reticence continues unchanged in Eastern Orthodox worship today. Something else happened to cause a profound change in European Christianity's understanding of salvation. Western theologians usually say that the greatest event in the development of salvation theology was the publication of the treatise "Why Did God Become Man?" by Anselm, the eleventh-century Archbishop of Canterbury. Before Anselm, as we've seen, the focus was on Christ's *victory* rather than on his *sufferings* as the means of salvation. "The wages of sin is Death," and due to our sins we were enslaved by death, poisoned and helpless to resist sin. Christ comes on a rescue mission, and in the process he suffers very much like that policeman rescuing the hostages. As a human, he dies and gains entrance to Hades; as God, he blasts it open and sets the captives free. It is in this sense—so Christians in the first millennium understood—that Scripture speaks of Christ's death as a ransom for many.

Some early writers elaborated on the question "Who received this ransom?," unwisely it would seem. Today their analogies seem crude—for example, that God lured the Devil by hiding Christ's divinity inside his humanity, and the Devil responded like a fish grabbing a baited hook (Gregory of Nyssa) or like a mouse going into a trap (Augustine).

But when we speak of Christ paying with his blood, we don't necessarily have to imagine a two-sided transaction. The brave policeman above "paid with his blood" to free the hostages, but that doesn't mean the kidnappers were left gloating over a vial of blood. When the Lord ransomed his people out of Egypt, Pharaoh did not accept a fat bag of gold in exchange. "Redeem" can just mean "doing what is necessary to set free."

Further, the young officer might have said, "I offer this mission to the honor of my chief, who has always been like a dad to me. I love him and want to do his will, and I am making this sacrifice in his name." The chief didn't receive the young man's blood either—a bizarre thought—nor did he require that blood before the hostages were freed; he was not their captor but rather an ally in the rescue. So take a step back and see these terms in a looser sense. Sometimes we use images like "paid" to mean a simple act of giving, without envisioning a two-sided transaction that includes a receiving on the other end.

Gregory of Nazianzus (fourth century) protested that the question of "Who received the payment?" should not be pressed hard. No matter what debt the Devil was owed, it could not possibly have included God himself. On the other hand, the Father could not have been the recipient of the ransom, since he was not the one holding us captive. And if the blood of Isaac had not pleased him, why would he desire the blood of his beloved son?

Nazianzus sums up: the Father accepts Christ's sacrifice without having demanded it; the Son offers it to honor him; and the result is the defeat of the Evil One. "This is as much as we shall say of Christ; the greater portion shall be reverenced with silence."

Anselm took aim at the exaggerated versions of the ransom theory, but he didn't agree to leave the greater portion to silence. He theorized that the payment *was* made to God the Father. In Anselm's formulation, our sins were like an offense against the honor of a mighty ruler. The ruler is not free to simply forgive the transgression; restitution must be made. This is perhaps the most crucial new element in the story; earlier Christians believed that God the Father did, in fact, freely forgive us, like the father of the Prodigal Son. No human would be adequate to pay this debt, so God the Son volunteered to do so. "If the Son chose to make over the claim He had on God to man, could the Father justly forbid Him doing so, or refuse to man what the Son willed to give him?" Christ satisfies our debt in this, the "satisfaction theory" of the atonement.

"And that has made all the difference," as a tousled Yankee poet liked to say. Western Christian theology marched on from that point, encountering controversies and developments and revisions, but locked on the idea that Christ's death was directed toward the Father. When Western theologians look back at the centuries before Anselm, they can't find his theory anywhere (well, there are some premonitions in Tertullian and Cyprian, but it wasn't the mainstream). But you can read St. Paul as supporting the "satisfaction" view, so Anselm is hailed as the first theologian to understand St. Paul.

That's a stretch, though. Would Christians really have misunderstood their salvation for a thousand years? Did the people Paul wrote his letters to have no idea what he was talking about? Did the early martyrs die without understanding the Cross that saved them? Why would the Holy Spirit permit such a thing, if he was sent to lead them into all truth? Is the "plain meaning of Scripture" so obscure that it couldn't be discerned for a thousand years, and then only by someone from a culture utterly different from that of its authors?

Before Anselm, the problem salvation addresses is seen as located within us. We are infected by Death as a result of Adam's fall. This infection will cause us to be spiritually sick and to commit sin, both voluntarily and as a result of the Devil's deceptions. Christ offers to rescue us in accord with the Father's will, like the young police officer above. In this action, God the Father and the Son are united: "God was in Christ reconciling the world to Himself."

That's the "before" snapshot. With Anselm, the problem salvation addresses is between us and God (we have a debt we can't pay). After Anselm it is even sometimes formulated as *within* God (His wrath won't be quenched until the debt is paid). This theory loses the unity of will between the Father and Son; it can appear that the Son has to overcome the Father's resistance. It loses the emphasis on the reality that the sickness is within us, and we need to be healed; it can appear that a legal acquittal is sufficient and a transformed life merely a nice afterthought.

Some rebelled against the Anselmian formulation and claimed that it was too legalistic, too ethically superficial, too "Old Testament." They proposed instead that Christ's sufferings are meant to move us by example, so that we will turn and be reconciled with God. (In response to a similar proposition many centuries earlier, Augustine had harrumphed that, if an example is all we needed, we didn't need Christ; the human condition would have been cleared up with Abel.)

In all these varied "after" snapshots, however, the wounds and suffering are the major point. It is the pain of the Passion that saves us, whether objectively (by paying a debt) or subjectively (by moving our hearts). From Julian of Norwich's meditations on the Crown of Thorns, to "O Sacred Head Sore Wounded," to Mel Gibson's *The Passion of the Christ* is a single devotional thread.

This is a strand that has produced powerfully affecting works of art and moved and inspired Christians for centuries. The Crucifixion was, in fact, bloody and brutal. Gibson is on good historical ground in wishing to depict it in this way—and when he prayerfully reads the Gospels, no doubt these are the pictures that appear in his mind.

But they are not, actually, there. The writers of the Gospels chose to describe Jesus' Passion a different way. Instead of evoking empathy they invite us to grateful, respectful awe, because they had a different understanding of the meaning of his suffering.

HIGH FIDELITY

(From *The Christian Century*)

Bill McKibben

I live in the north country mountains, where winter begins in late October and gives up, some years, in early May. That means you come to church half the year in boots—heavy boots, in case you get stuck in a snowbank on the way. Which means, in turn, that the carpet on the floor better be some shade of brown.

Two or three times in my years there I've vacuumed the church. (Not very often, because we tend to divide up jobs along Traditional Gender Lines. Men make sure the furnace is turned up, change the storm windows, lift heavy things, paint, put away folding chairs, shovel the stairs. Women do everything else.) The first time I vacuumed I was merrily buzzing away between the pews, listening to the random click-clack of sand disappearing up the hose, when all of a sudden the noise trebled—click-click-click, like a Geiger counter in a uranium mine.

At that moment I was vacuuming beneath the third pew right along the center aisle. Right where Frank and Jean have been sitting every single Sunday that I can remember. I believe that Frank and Jean began attending our congregation the Sunday after the Council of Nicea. Each time they claim the same spot.

I kept vacuuming, hoovering up the same steady background level of sand, until I reached the sixth pew, against the right wall, where Velda and Don sit each Sunday—each Sunday they possibly can, that is, as both of them have been as much in the hospital as out lately. Again my Geiger counter went off. I decided that instead of radioactivity, it was measuring something else. Fidelity.

"Spirituality" is our watchword at the moment, of course. And rightly so. But Woody Allen had a point when he said that 90 percent of life consists in just showing up.

Consider what it means to belong to the same rural Methodist church for sixty or seventy years. Because Methodist central command insists on changing preachers about as frequently as Sheraton changes sheets, and because small, poor, rural congregations serve as practice ground for the rawest seminary graduates, anyone sitting in the pews for a decade or two sees a head-spinning mix of styles, theologies, and talents.

When I first arrived, the incumbent pastor was a jailhouse convert—a holy roller with a pinkie ring who returned whence he had come after embezzling a widow's insurance. Since then we've had wonderful people in the pulpit—some conservatives, some progressives. Some of them illustrated their sermons with examples taken from some preacher's helper that must have been published in 1921 because the anecdotes all involved World War I. We've taken communion by every method short of scuba diving into a tank of wine. We had one truly great preacher. She was young, smart, funny, full of love, able to talk to young and old, able to afflict the few of us who were comfortable while simultaneously comforting the many afflicted. And she hadn't been there a month before we were, all of us, worried sick about what it was going to be like when, inevitably, she would have to leave. Though none of us would have traded her years for anything, in certain ways it was the hardest passage of all.

Through it all Don and Velda and Frank and Jean never wavered. They might not have liked some new theological twist or liturgical gambit, but they didn't complain very much. (Not even when every other pastor would reinstitute the Greeting of the Neighbors, or the Passing of the Peace, or whatever they called it—a practice that makes less sense when the same fifteen people are there every week, and you've greeted them when you came in, and you're going to greet them again at coffee hour.) And they kept doing the fairly awesome amount of labor even a poor small church requires if it is to keep going.

It's easy to say that all this doesn't add up to a daring relationship with God, that it's Mary and Martha come to life, that routine can suck the meaning out of something as bracing as the gospel. But those of us who've claimed this place were attracted by the sheer dogged devotion of the regulars.

My generation has been good at many things, but tenacity—faithfulness—is not one of them. Sometimes, in fact, we simply want too much. Like marriages that complete us, fulfill us in every way, make us whole, instead of marriages where, on most days, it's enough to be living faithfully together, adding another increment of quotidian devotion, giving each other the benefit of the doubt. Or like religious *experiences*, instead of the experience of being religious. I have no real sense of what it might have felt like to inhabit the medieval world, when the church was simply the air one breathed, the environment in which one lived. Or rather, what sense of that world I have comes from watching people like Frank and Jean and Don and Velda.

One spring day some years ago, when Don and I had finished taking down the storm windows, we decided to climb up into the steeple on a rickety ladder so that we could take in the view across our small town. We could see the house where he'd grown up, and the graveyard where many generations of his ancestors were buried. And while we were up there Don showed me something else—the place he had carved his initials, and Velda's. Sometime in the 1920s, when they were in grade school.

CONFESSIONS OF
A TRAVELING CALVINIST

Richard J. Mouw

I once proposed an interesting little exercise to a small group of evangelical Christians. I asked them to think of a young woman they cared deeply about but who was not a Christian. Suppose you could make it happen that this young woman would spend several days of relaxed time with a well-known Christian leader who would talk with her about her relationship with God. Whom would you choose from the list I'm giving you? Then I gave them evangelical names they were familiar with, all either television evangelists or prominent theologians. But I also included two Roman Catholics—the priest Henri Nouwen and Mother Teresa (both of whom were alive at the time). I wasn't surprised at their choices. They all chose one of the two Catholics.

This experiment demonstrated two things to all of us: first, that our evangelical attitudes toward Roman Catholicism had changed significantly in recent years, and second, that when it comes down to someone we love dearly who is not a Christian, what many of us care about most is that they see living examples of what it means to have a warm, trusting relationship with Jesus. The evangelists and theologians I put on the list were respected as folks who might have articulated the right verbal message, but the group did not see them as folks who would effectively communicate the love of Jesus to the young woman. For this the group looked to people like Nouwen and Mother Teresa (and, I am sure, Billy Graham, if I had included him as a candidate).

I have a strong suspicion that my grandmother would not approve of my thoughts and sentiments on this point. Here I simply have to say that her experience was rather limited. I love to return in my spirit to the villages of my ancestors, and I want to remain loyal to their basic theological convictions. But I have had to rework their theology in the light of what I experience as a Christian who is forced to think ecumenically and globally on a daily basis. I have learned too much from the inhabitants of other villages to ever fit neatly into their Dutch village life. I have been taught by the residents of monasteries and convents, slums in Mexico City, black townships in South Africa, Jewish ghettos in Eastern Europe, Amish farming settlements in Manitoba, and refugee camps in the Middle East. So while Sliedrecht and Dordrecht continue to be spiritual landmarks for me when I return there for spiritual and theological nurture, I know I carry lessons and loyalties with me that would not have pleased either my grandmother or the learned churchmen who gathered at the seventeenth-century Synod of Dordt.

"Nearly Perfect" Christianity?

Recently I read a book about Calvinism written in the 1920s. The author, R. B. Kuiper, was an old-fashioned Calvinist who liked to set forth rather bold claims on behalf of the system of thought he was defending. "Calvinism," he wrote, "is the most nearly perfect interpretation of Christianity. In the final analysis Calvinism and Christianity are practically synonymous." And to reinforce his point he quoted a similar sentiment from the great nineteenth-century Princeton theologian Benjamin Warfield: "Calvinism is just religion in its purity. We have only, therefore, to conceive of religion in its purity, and that is Calvinism."[1]

I have to admit that when I read remarks of this sort on behalf of Calvinism, I usually cringe a little. They strike me as claiming too much on Calvinism's behalf. But in this case my reaction was not so negative, because two pages earlier R. B. Kuiper had set the stage for his seemingly bold claims with a more modest statement. Even "the most ardent Calvinist," he wrote, "can hardly maintain that his interpretation of the Christian religion is perfectly full-orbed, and that no other interpretation contains aught to supplement it."[2]

In what sense, then, did the author believe that Calvinism is the "nearly perfect" interpretation of Christianity? Well, not in the sense that only Calvinists are true Christians. He was making a much more charitable point, namely, that all true Christians are, whether they know it or not, Calvinists at heart. A person, he says, "may not call himself a Calvinist; he may even resent being called by this name"—but that's what he is "in the final analysis" if he "lives in utter dependence upon God."[3]

This is not unlike the view of Calvinism that Charles Spurgeon endorsed when he said that if anyone would ask him what he means when he calls himself a Calvinist, he would respond that a Calvinist is someone who says, *Salvation is of the Lord.* In saying this, Spurgeon was not insisting that only a Calvinist truly believes that salvation can only come from a sovereign God. He was expressing a confidence that everyone—whatever the theological system to which a person explicitly subscribes—who genuinely experiences a total dependence on divine mercy for their salvation is a Calvinist in spirit.

I have much sympathy for this way of putting it. But I am still reluctant to say this kind of thing myself. For one thing, it seems a bit condescending. The Jesuit theologian Karl Rahner once argued that there are people in non-Christian religions who are "anonymous Christians."[4] By this he meant that some Muslims or Hindus might actually be motivated by a genuine Christlike spirit, even though they would never claim to adhere to uniquely Christian teachings. But this way of stating the case did not always go over well with scholars representing other religious traditions. They complained that the "anonymous Christian" label was an expression of Christian arrogance; they wanted to be taken seriously for what they actually said they believed *as* Hindus or Muslims. I have the same sense about proclaiming my Methodist or Catholic friends to be "anonymous Calvinists."

But I also think that designating all true Christians as Calvinists claims more for Calvinism than we have a right to claim. I am firmly convinced that Calvinism is right about some extremely important matters of faith. I am not prepared, however, to say with Warfield that "Calvinism is just religion in its purity"—mainly because I don't think that Calvinism really does justice to many dimensions of Christian discipleship.

An Embarrassing Weakness

One area, for example, where I believe Calvinism has been embarrassingly weak is in ethics—an important part of the Christian life for any perspective that claims to be, in

Warfield's words, "religion in its purity." Calvinists have certainly not stood out in the Christian community as especially pure people when it comes to the way they behave. They have frequently been intolerant, sometimes to the point of taking abusive and violent action toward people with whom they have disagreed. They have often promoted racist policies. And the fact that they have often defended these things by appealing directly to Calvinist teachings suggests that at least something in these patterns may be due to some weaknesses in the Calvinist perspective itself. On such matters, it seems clear to me that Calvinists ought to repent and admit to the larger Christian community that we have much to learn from others—from Mennonites, from black members of South African Pentecostal churches, from the followers of Saint Francis, and many others.

If nowhere else, then at least on ethical matters, Calvinists could stand to develop considerable humility. John Calvin himself lifted up humility as a central virtue. He makes this observation:

> A saying of Chrysostom's has always pleased me very much, that the foundation of our philosophy is humility. But that of Augustine pleases me even more: "When a certain rhetorician was asked what was the chief rule in eloquence, he replied, 'Delivery'; what was the second rule, 'Delivery'; what was the third rule, 'Delivery'; so if you ask me concerning the precepts of the Christian religion, first, second, third, and always I would answer, 'Humility.'"[5]

Humility is an important virtue to cultivate in dealing with the basic issues of the Christian life. And when it comes to ethical issues, Calvinists would do well to cultivate this virtue in large doses.

A Desire to Learn from Others

But, of course, humility by itself is not enough. After all, a group of people could decide to be humble about the fact that they alone possess the truth about the basic issues of life! This sort of humility can at best produce an attitude of tolerance toward all the other misguided souls in the world. I prefer a theological humility that is coupled with a genuine desire to *learn from others*.

I have learned so much from other Christian traditions that I have come to think of myself as an *eclectic* Calvinist. I draw freely from other traditions in fleshing out my theology. I do not see my Calvinism as locking me into a closed system of thought that must resist at all costs any outside theological influences.

And this should be expected, because Calvinism as such cannot survive as a closed system. "Mere Calvinism," as summarized in the TULIP doctrines—total depravity; unconditional election; limited atonement; irresistible grace; perseverance of the saints—does not cover a wide enough theological territory to serve in this way. The TULIP doctrines address the fundamentally important question of how an individual gets right with God. But the answer to this question—of which TULIP is a summary—does not a whole theology make.

"Mere Calvinism" *needs* fleshing out—and Calvinists have done so in many different ways. If you were to gather together a cross section of people who enthusiastically agree with each other about TULIP, you would find that they nonetheless disagree on a number of other important theological questions. Anglican Calvinists' doctrine of the church differs from that of Congregational Calvinists. Baptist and Reformed Calvinists argue about adult baptism versus infant baptism. And even within each of these groups people debate questions about the proper methods of evangelism, the best way to understand the Lord's Supper, questions about ordination, how best to relate to the larger culture, and so on. Once we get beyond the TULIP doctrines, then, Calvinism itself is a theologically diverse movement.

But when I admit to being eclectic, I am making more than the obvious point—that "mere Calvinism" does not by itself give us a doctrine of the church, the sacraments, and so on. I don't just learn from Calvinists who have fleshed out the TULIP doctrines in different ways. I have found it helpful, even necessary, to learn from theological perspectives that pose alternative answers to those of the TULIP doctrines themselves.

Learning from Diversity

Someone once asked me, "How can a Calvinist like you survive—especially as the president!—at a school as diverse as Fuller Theological Seminary?" I wish I would have asked her which part she found most puzzling: that I could tolerate Fuller's diversity, or that Fuller could tolerate my Calvinism!

For my part, I have to say that I thrive on the interaction. You don't hang around at a place like Fuller Seminar simply to keep your theological perspective intact; for that you're better off looking for another place to hang out. At any given time, Fuller's student body and faculty represent about seventy nations and approximately 120 denominations. Some of us come from Calvinist traditions, but we also have Wesleyans, Pentecostals, "new wave charismatics," Lutherans, Anglicans, and many others—including increasing numbers of Roman Catholics and Orthodox who have strong sympathies with evangelical Protestantism. And, of course, the cultural diversity makes for theological differences as well: a Korean Presbyterian is different from a Presbyterian from Nebraska, a Nigerian Anglican from his Australian Anglican counterpart, and so on.

Being exposed on a daily basis to the rich diversity of the body of Christ has taught me to look at more than the theology a person professes in judging his or her value to the kingdom of God. On this point I take encouragement from the way Charles Spurgeon defended John Wesley against the criticisms lodged by many of the Calvinists of Spurgeon's day. "While I detest many of the doctrines which he preached," wrote Spurgeon, "yet for the man himself I have a reverence second to no Wesleyan." He went on to comment as follows:

> The character of John Wesley stands beyond all imputation for self-sacrifice, zeal, holiness, and communion with God; he lived far above the ordinary level of common Christians, and was one "of whom the world was not worthy." I believe there are multitudes of men who cannot see these [Calvinistic] truths, or, at least, cannot see them in the way in which we put them, who nevertheless have received Christ as their Savior, and are as dear to the heart of the God of grace as the soundest Calvinist in or out of Heaven.[6]

I am less inclined than Spurgeon to use a word like "detest" in describing my disagreement with many other evangelicals on important points of doctrine. But in this case I am glad he used that word, since it makes the contrast with his warm comments about Wesley's godliness even more impressive.

Spurgeon clearly believed that John Wesley loved the same gospel Calvinists love. In whatever way some of Wesley's theological formulations might have differed from those of Calvinist thought, there should be no doubt that he saw himself as a sinner who was totally dependent on sovereign grace for his salvation. I like Surgeon's charitable spirit. Rather than insisting that only Calvinists are genuine Christians, I prefer to think that Calvinism best captures experiences and concerns that are at work in the lives of everyone who knows what it's like to plead for divine mercy out of a recognition of our own unworthiness.

Doctrine is very important. But it is not everything. Like Spurgeon, I stand in awe of the deep commitment to Christ I see in people whose professed theology often makes me quite nervous.

Being Open to Correction

But my openness to people whose theology is different from my own goes further than simply respecting them for their godly lives. I have also learned much from folks who do not share my Calvinist convictions. From them I have learned to see important *correctives* in other theological perspectives. For example, as a Calvinist I clearly want to place a strong emphasis on divine sovereignty. Indeed, we Calvinists are so single-minded in this that if we are ever faced with a choice between a theological formulation that diminishes God's sovereignty and one that would diminish human freedom, we'll go with sovereignty. We would rather err on the side of underemphasizing human responsibility than to detract in any way from the sovereign rule of God over all things.

Most other theological perspectives place a greater emphasis on human freedom. In doing so, they often give the impression that God is limited by our human choices. Needless to say, this sort of thing makes me nervous. But I also see tendencies in my own Calvinism that make me nervous. Christians who specialize in free-will-centered theologies, for example, typically do a much better job at evangelism than Calvinists do. I believe that evangelism is extremely important. Rather than simply railing away at the alleged errors of those other theologies, then, I find it most helpful to look at the correctives they are supplying for Calvinists like me.

Getting a Second Opinion

The other category of lessons I learned has to do with what I see as the need to recognize a variety of theological *specializations.* I find it helpful to see some of the theological differences that exist in the Christian community as stemming from something like the different specialized areas of expertise we see in the medical profession. Some physicians focus primarily on preventative medicine, others on correcting existing problems. Some incline toward surgical solutions, while others generally prefer noninvasive strategies.

In the big picture, all of these medical specializations have their place. This is why it's always important to consider getting a second opinion when dealing with a medical problem. And in weighing conflicting professional recommendations, it is necessary to take the specializations of the recommenders into account.

The world of theology also has its specializations. This was brought home in a very practical way during my student days when I had a teacher who was a committed Christian pacifist. I was very fond of him as a teacher, but I did not agree with his pacifist views and I would often stay after class to argue with him. He was a gentle man, and he patiently dealt with my objections to his views. One day I rather passionately threw out a challenge that pacifists are accustomed to hearing. "Suppose the Communists came to your home," I asked, "and threatened to kill you and your whole family, and suppose you had a chance to stop them by using violence—wouldn't you forsake your pacifist principles in that kind of situation?" He replied by saying that even then he would not use violence. "Why not?" I asked. "Because killing us is not the worst thing they could do to me and my loved ones," he answered. "Well, what is the worst thing?" I shot back. I have never forgotten his response: "The worst thing any human being could do to me and my family is to separate us from the love of Jesus. But I know that no human being can really do that." And then he quoted from memory the wonderful passage from Romans 8:

> For I am persuaded, that neither death, nor life, nor angels, nor principalities, nor powers, nor things present, nor things to come, nor height, nor depth, nor any other creature, shall be able to separate us from the love of God, which is in Christ Jesus our Lord [Romans 8:38–39, KJV].

I never became the pacifist he would have liked me to be. But I've never forgotten the lesson he taught me. My own willingness to endorse the use of violence in many real-life situations is, as I see it, correct. But it is also dangerous. I risk the danger—and my pattern of questioning to him was evidence of this—that I will lean toward putting my ultimate trust in violent means of protection. His answer reminded me of something I was not inclined to be sensitive to in dealing with the hypothetical case I was presenting, namely, that our only real safety must be found in God, and that the worst thing that can happen to a human being is to be cut off from this source of safety. My teacher saw this more clearly than I did because he *specialized* in thinking about matters of ultimate "defense."

When I encounter what looks like a deep theological difference, I try to remind myself to ask what specialization might be at work in the other person's way of viewing things, and how I might learn from it. I realize that many other Christians—including probably most Calvinists—will find this to be a rather messy way of dealing with theological differences. But I have also learned to allow for a certain degree of messiness in my theology.

Puzzles and Mysteries

I like the description of the theological task given by a British monk named Thomas Weinandy. He says we should not think of theology primarily as a problem-solving activity. Rather, it is best understood as "a mystery-discerning enterprise." When we solve a problem, all of our puzzles disappear, and this is not what we should normally expect in theological exploration. The most we can usually hope for when we think carefully about a theological topic, he says, is to see "more precisely and clearly what the mystery is."[7]

This seems right to me. While I love the TULIP doctrines, I know they don't make many puzzles go away. But they do help me discern the mysteries of how a sovereign God draws rebel sinners to himself, restoring them to the purposes for which they were originally created. I try to keep a primary focus on that set of mysteries. But I have to realize that I also need a lot of theological help from Christians who have cultivated some rather different theological specializations.

Notes

1. R. B. Kuiper, *As to Being Reformed* (Grand Rapids, Mich.: Eerdmans, 1926), 88. The Warfield comment is from Benjamin Warfield, "What Is Calvinism?" in *Benjamin B. Warfield: Selected Shorter Writings,* vol. 1, ed. John E. Meeter (Phillipsburg, N.J.: Presbyterian & Reformed Publishing, 1970), 389.
2. Kuiper, *As to Being Reformed,* 86.
3. Kuiper, *As to Being Reformed,* 92.
4. See Karl Rahner, "Anonymous Christians," in *Theological Investigations,* vol. 6 (Baltimore, Md.: Helicon, 1969), 390–398.
5. John Calvin, *Institutes of the Christian Religion,* ed. John T. McNeill, trans. Ford Lewis Battles (Philadelphia: Westminster, 1960), 2.2.11, 268–269.
6. Charles Spurgeon, "A Defense of Calvinism," www.spurgeon.org/calvinis.htm.
7. Thomas G. Weinandy, O.F.M., Cap., *Does God Suffer?* (Notre Dame, Ind.: University of Notre Dame Press, 2000), 32–34.

THE PERSISTENCE OF
THE CATHOLIC MOMENT

(From *First Things*)

Richard John Neuhaus

In 1987, while I was still a Lutheran, I published a book titled *The Catholic Moment: The Paradox of the Church in the Postmodern World.* There I argued that the Catholic Church is the leading and indispensable community in advancing the Christian movement in world history. In evangelization, in furthering the Christian intellectual tradition, in the quest for Christian unity, in advocating the culture of life, and in every other aspect of the Christian mission, this was, I contended, the Catholic Moment. I am frequently asked whether I still believe that, or whether the Moment has been missed, or derailed, or simply delayed. The short answer is: if the Catholic Church is what she claims to be—and about that I have no doubt—then every moment from Pentecost to Our Lord's return in glory is the Catholic Moment. But the degree to which that Moment is realized in the little span of time that is ours depends on whether contemporary Catholicism has the nerve to be fully and distinctively Catholic.

To be Catholic is not a private preference but a matter of ordering one's loves and loyalties to the very public communal reality that is the Catholic Church. For others, religion may be what a person does with his solitude, or what people do together with their solitudes, but Catholicism is a corporate reality. It is what Catholics used to call a "perfect society" within the imperfect societies of the world, or what Vatican II, with essentially the same intention, calls the People of God. It understands itself to be an apostolically constituted community, and its distinguishing mark is communion with the Bishop of Rome who, alone of religious leaders in the world—and this is a matter of the greatest symbolic and practical significance—is not a citizen or subject of any temporal sovereignty.

It is suggested by some that the public influence of Catholicism has been greatly weakened, not least by the scandals of the past year. The question of Catholicism in the public square, however, is not—at least not chiefly—the question of Catholic influence in social change or public policy, never mind electoral politics. Catholicism in the public square is a matter of being, fully and vibrantly, the public community that is the Catholic Church. More than by recent scandals, Catholicism in the public square is weakened by its gradual but certain sociological accommodation to a Protestant ethos—also in its secularized forms—that construes religion in terms of consumer preference and voluntary associations in support of those preferences. It is weakened also by what is aptly called the totalitarian impulse of the modern state—including democratic states—to monopolize public space and consign religion to the private sphere, thus producing what I have called the naked public square.

The second dynamic is evident on several fronts and is now at crisis level in Catholic education, especially higher education, and in health care. At issue is the freedom of the Church to govern herself. It is not enough that there be a flourishing network of voluntary associations called Catholic parishes confined to doing religious things on Sunday morning and other appointed times. That is not what the Second Vatican Council meant by the apostolically constituted public society called the People of God. The great Catholic battle of the modern era has been for *libertas ecclesiae*—the liberty of the Church to govern herself. In America today, for reasons both internal and external to the life of the Church, that battle is being lost on some fronts.

In many ways, Catholicism in America is flourishing. It is far and away the fastest growing religious community in the country, with almost two hundred thousand adult converts per year, and patterns of immigration and youthful adherence that will likely expand its numbers far beyond the present sixty-three million. Contrary to the fears of some, and the hopes of others, there is no evidence that the events of the past year will impede this growth. In this country and worldwide, the two most vibrant and growing sectors of the two-billion-plus Christian movement are Catholicism and evangelical/pentecostal Protestantism. John Paul II speaks of the new millennium as a "springtime of evangelization," and there is reason to believe that is much more than wishful thinking. In this country and elsewhere, we witness the beginnings of historic convergences between Catholics and evangelicals. Such cultural and moral convergences are not without political consequences, but more important are the spiritual and theological convergences that could reshape the Christian reality in the century ahead. (In this connection, I warmly recommend a careful reading of Philip Jenkins's recent book, *The Next Christendom.*) So Catholicism is flourishing. The question is, with specific reference to America, how and in what ways will Catholicism be vibrantly, or even recognizably, Catholic?

Three years ago, marking the seventy-fifth anniversary of *Commonweal* magazine, its former editor Peter Steinfels wrote an article that is, I believe, both wise and courageous: "Reinventing Liberal Catholicism: Between Powerful Enemies and Dubious Allies." Since the dawn of modernity, said Steinfels, liberal Catholicism has been marked by several characteristics: a devotion to *libertas ecclesiae;* an eagerness to critically engage the culture; an understanding that the Church is in history and therefore necessarily involved in change and development; a devotion to unfettered intellectual inquiry; a recognition of the integrity and autonomy of distinct spheres of human activity; and an interest in reforming the structures of the Church in support of her apostolic mission through time. Heroes of this liberal Catholicism, according to Steinfels, are such as John Henry Newman and Jacques Maritain. If this depiction of liberal Catholicism is accurate, we should all want to call ourselves liberal Catholics. Which is another way of saying that, although Mr. Steinfels and others may have problems with this, we should be John Paul II Catholics.

Liberal Catholics, says Steinfels, have been riding high since the Council; they have largely defined what is meant by the "post–Vatican II Church." But now they are facing the "powerful enemies" mentioned in his subtitle, and, in this pontificate, liberal Catholics are viewed as suspect by Rome. "The most obvious and fundamental working difference between these [enemy] groups and liberal Catholics," he writes, "turns on the possibility that the pope, despite the guidance of the Holy Spirit, might be subject to tragic error. Liberal Catholics believe that this possibility, which all Catholics recognize as historical fact, did not conveniently disappear at some point in the distant past, like 1950, but was probably the case in the 1968 issuance of *Humanae Vitae* and cannot be ruled out in the refusal of ordination to women."

To which this liberal Catholic (as defined above) responds that of course this pope can and has made mistakes. But what is now called liberal Catholicism is besieged and suspect because of its refusal to honestly receive the teachings of Vatican II as authoritatively interpreted by the Magisterium, and not least by the pontificate of John Paul II. Liberal Catholics joined with what Steinfels calls their "dubious allies" on the left in claiming that Vatican II called for a revolution, and they acted accordingly. It is now obvious that it was a revolution that was not to be. The now-failing revolution predictably provoked reactions of retrenchment, resulting in the toxic discontents of both right and left in American Catholicism. What has not been received, what has not been embraced, what has not been internalized, what has not been tried is the bold proposal of renewal and reform advanced by John Paul II. Although the future of the proposal is uncertain, those bishops who have in recent months been calling for a plenary council in the United States to solemnly receive the Second Vatican Council and its authoritative interpretation are, it seems to me, exactly right. The way forward is the way of the Council that was and is. Thirty-seven years is enough, and more than enough, of bitter contention over the imagined Vatican II of leftist enthusiasms and rightist fears.

For decades, the Catholic left has called for a Vatican Council III to "complete" the work of Vatican II. Others on the left, such as Garry Wills, dissent from that call, claiming that Vatican II put the teaching magisterium out of business once and for all, "diffusing" ecclesial authority throughout the Spirit-guided private opinions of the People of God. This move is implausibly presented as what is meant by the *sensus fidelium*. The burden of Steinfels's argument is that liberal Catholicism made a great mistake since the Council in not distinguishing itself and, when necessary, separating itself, from its "dubious allies" of the Catholic left. Turning from its intellectual and theological tasks, liberalism got bogged down in the canonical litany of leftist complaints about contraception, homosexuality, women's ordination, and clerical celibacy, along with endless agitations aimed at "power sharing" in church government—and all of these linked to the larger question of papal teaching authority. Moreover, sectors of the Catholic left became increasingly part of a political and cultural left that is increasingly secularist and post-Christian, and even explicitly anti-Christian. Liberal Catholics, says Steinfels, should have made it clear that, in very important respects, these dubious allies of the Catholic left were not allies at all.

The association with the Catholic left created, he wrote, a crisis of irony, a crisis of intellect, and a crisis of inclusiveness. The absence of irony and historical perspective led to fanaticism and a sectarian spirit. The refusal to make serious arguments nurtured anti-intellectualism and an emphasis on an ever-expanding inclusiveness which emphatically excluded those not of like mind and resulted in a loss of Catholic identity. The Catholic left, he says, has no patience with liberalism's devotion to "compromise, incrementalism, or extended analysis and debate." "The Catholic left," he writes, "is an offspring of liberal Catholicism, but is rooted in the dramatic appeals and confrontations of the 1960s" rather than the liberal, and mainly European, tradition of the nineteenth and twentieth centuries. But so smugly triumphalistic were liberals following the Council, while at the same time—and somewhat contradictorily—so fearful of their "powerful enemies" on the right, that few were, and few are, prepared to challenge the dubious alliance with the Catholic left. The old maxim applied: the enemy of my enemies . . .

Steinfels's point about Catholic identity is of particular importance. One has waited for a long time for a persuasive answer to the question of why, if the canonical litany of left-liberal demands were met, Catholicism would not be very much like oldline liberal Protestantism. Perhaps like the Episcopal Church, except very much bigger and with shabbier liturgical practices. The Catholic left has little interest in, or capacity for, addressing the question of what makes Catholicism distinctively Catholic, and liberal Catholics have not called them to account on that score. With respect to Catholic identity, Steinfels writes, the attitude on the left takes the form of the question, "Isn't [the question of what is authentically Catholic], after all, a task we can leave to church authorities, whom we will then feel free to criticize?"

There is among cradle Catholics of a left-liberal bent—and perhaps this is more evident to those who come into the Church later in life—an astonishing insouciance about the solidity and perdurance of Catholicism. Catholic identity, what makes Catholicism Catholic, is a question that will take care of itself or is somebody else's worry. It is not our job, they seem to be saying, to maintain the ecclesiastical playground in which we pursue our deconstructive games. This apparent insouciance may be a form of unshakable faith in the promise that the gates of hell shall not prevail. But I think not. Rather, it seems to me, this insouciance—or to call it by another name, this recklessness—reflects an ecclesiastical fundamentalism that is akin to the Bible fundamentalism of some other Christians. It is indifferent to the incarnational reality of a Church subject to the trials, testings, distortions, inspirations, and mistakes of history. I do believe that the gates of hell shall not prevail against the Church, but the ravages of the reckless confidence that no serious harm is done by unbounded criticism, conflict, and contradiction should not be ignored. There is the harm of souls misled—and possibly lost—of intellectual and artistic traditions trashed, and of innumerable persons denied the high adventure of Catholic fidelity.

I recently had occasion to reread Jacques Maritain's *The Peasant of the Garonne,* a book written in the months immediately following the conclusion of Vatican II in December 1965. Critics at the time called it a cranky book of disillusioned hopes, and there is truth in that; but it is also a stunningly prescient book that recognized what might be termed the hijacking of liberal Catholicism and its long-term consequences. As a liberal, Maritain had no illusions about what came to be called the "the pre-Vatican II church." He knows about the anti-intellectualism, the suspicion of scholarship and science, and the stifling juridicalism of disciplinary measures. "All this," he writes, "was going to build up, in the unconscious of a great many Christians, clerics and laymen, an enormous weight of frustration, disillusionment, repressed doubts, resentment, bitterness, healthy desires sacrificed, with all the anxieties and pent-up aspirations of the unhappy conscience. Comes the *aggiornamento.* Why be astonished that at the very announcement of a Council, then in the surrounding of it, and now after it, the enormous unconscious weight which I have just mentioned burst into the open in a kind of explosion that does no honor to the human intelligence?" The explosive reaction to the earlier repression, says Maritain, resulted in interpretations of the Council marked by a "kneeling to the world." He leaves no doubt that he believes these interpretations are, in fact, misinterpretations—sometimes innocent, sometimes deliberate. As for the Council itself, it "appears as an island guarded by the Spirit of God in the middle of a stormy ocean that is overturning everything, the true and the false."

The storm and its aftermath were powerfully evident a few years later in events surrounding *Humanae Vitae,* the 1968 encyclical on human sexuality. That moment marks, among other things, the point at which bishops largely— albeit in most cases inadvertently—surrendered their role as teachers. An orchestrated campaign of theologians and other academics publicly rejected a solemn magisterial pronouncement on faith and morals, and the world held its breath to see what would happen. A few bishops tried to impose discipline, but they were not supported by Rome, and the result was that nothing happened. Except that it was now established in the minds of many that the Church pretends to teach with authority, but bishops, theologians, priests, and the faithful are free to ignore what is taught.

Humanae Vitae, it is important to underscore, does not stand alone. The teaching that the conjugal act of love should be open to new life and not be negated by contraceptive means is deeply rooted in centuries of tradition. *Humanae Vitae* reaffirmed that tradition, as did Pius XI when it was first thrown into question in 1930, and as has every pontificate since then. There is, I would suggest, no new argument that has not been addressed in papal teaching. It is true but entirely beside the point that most Catholics do not adhere to the teaching; most Catholics have never had the teaching explained to them in a manner that invites their assent. It is simply not plausible that liberal Catholics such as Newman and Maritain would not affirm that this teaching of the Church is binding upon the Catholic conscience.

Critiques of liberal Catholicism—where it went wrong and how it might be set right—such as that offered by Peter Steinfels are to be warmly welcomed. The concern for Catholic identity is on the mark, but I suggest that no identity is recognizably Catholic if it skirts the question of obedience. Here, too, we need the intellectual honesty and civil discussion for which Steinfels calls. We need to revive what Newman called "the grammar of assent" in recognizing that, on controverted questions such as artificial contraception and the Church's inability to ordain women, the Church calls for the obedience of external and internal assent. I know that intellectual obedience is a scandalous idea in our time. And not only in our time, for it has been a stumbling block to many over the centuries. What is sometimes called "ecclesial faith," as distinct from "divine faith" or "religious submission," is an inseparable part of what it means to be Catholic, of what it means for our loves and allegiances to be rightly ordered. Contrary to modern doctrines of autonomy, there is nothing demeaning about obedience. The word is from the Latin *ob-audire* and means "to give ear to, to listen to, to follow guidance."

Accepting full intellectual and moral responsibility for his decision, the Catholic decides whom to listen to, whom to follow, and, come the crunch, to whom to submit. The Catholic believes that, in the apostolically constituted community of faith, the Bishop of Rome is Peter among us. The Catholic believes that the words of Jesus, "He who hears you hears me," have abiding historical applicability until the end of time. The bishops teaching "with and under" Peter can teach infallibly. Infallibility means that the fullness of apostolic authority will never be invoked to require us to believe anything that is false. The relationship between freedom and faith is set forth in Vatican II's *Constitution on the Church in the Modern World:*

It is only in freedom, however, that human beings can turn to what is good, and our contemporaries are right in highly praising and assiduously pursuing such freedom, although often they do so in wrong ways as if it gave a license to do anything one pleases, even evil. Genuine freedom is an outstanding sign of the divine image in human beings. . . . Human dignity demands that the individual act according to a knowing and free choice, as motivated and prompted personally from within, and not through blind internal impulse or merely external pressure.

I may not understand an authoritative teaching of the Magisterium, I may have difficulties with a teaching, but, as Newman understood, a thousand difficulties do not add up to a doubt, never mind a rejection. I may think a teaching is inadequately expressed, and pray and work for its more adequate expression in the future. But, given a decision between what I think the Church should teach and what the Church in fact does teach, I decide for the Church. I decide freely and rationally—because God has promised the apostolic leadership of the Church guidance and charisms that He has not promised me; because I think the Magisterium just may understand some things that I don't; because I know for sure that, in the larger picture of history, the witness of the Catholic Church is immeasurably more important than anything I might think or say. In short, I obey. The nuances of such obedience, of what is meant by "thinking with the Church" (*sentire cum ecclesia*), are admirably spelled out in the 1990 instruction of the Congregation for the Doctrine of the Faith, "The Ecclesial Vocation of the Theologian." It is an instruction that can be read with enormous benefit also by those who are not professional theologians. My point is this: liberal Catholicism cannot be reinvented, it cannot be rehabilitated, it will not be vibrantly Catholic, until it candidly and convincingly comes to terms with obedience.

The great question, a question that has ramifications that go far beyond assent to Catholic teaching, is the relationship between freedom and obedience—or, more precisely, between freedom and truth. The question includes ecclesial obedience to the truth, as Catholics believe the truth is made known. We are bound by the truth, and when we are bound by the truth, we are bound to be free. The relationship between truth and freedom is as true for non-Catholics or, indeed, for non-Christians as it is true for Catholics, as is magnificently argued by John Paul II in *Veritatis Splendor* (The Splendor of Truth). What went wrong with aspects of liberal Catholicism has its roots in what went wrong long before the 1960s. What went wrong was the submission to an Enlightenment or rationalist tradition—found also in a romanticism that too often mirrored what it intended to counter—of the autonomous self. Still today there is a liberal Catholic reflex, shared by secular liberalism, against the very ideas of authority, obedience, and the truth that binds. The Catholic insight about human freedom, an insight that we dare to say has universal applicability, is that we are bound to be free. The truth, in order to be understood, must be loved, and love binds. And so also with the apostolic community that embodies and articulates the truth.

Coming to terms with the question of obedience means coming to terms with the one who said, "If you continue in my word, you are truly my disciples, and you will know the truth, and the truth will make you free." The modern regime of secular liberalism adopted the slogan "The truth will make you free," but pitted it against the one who is the truth. More radically, it pitted truth and freedom against any authoritative statement of truth, and against authority itself. The liberal ideal was that of the autonomous, untethered, unencumbered self. The consequence of that impossible ideal is conformism to the delusion of autonomy or, as the history of the last century so tragically demonstrates, blind submission to totalitarian doctrines that present themselves as surrogates for the truth that makes us free.

The "dubious ally" that has done in liberal Catholicism again and again is the conceptual regime of secular liberalism, and its misconstrual of the connection between freedom and truth. The result is liberal Catholics who insist that they belong—"Once a Catholic, always a Catholic"—but it is a belonging without being bound. Let it be admitted that this is true of all of us—in different ways, and to a greater or lesser extent. There is perhaps no greater obstacle to our entering upon the high adventure of Catholic fidelity than modernity's perverse idea of freedom, an idea that we breathe with the cultural air that surrounds us. And there is important truth in the maxim "Once a Catholic, always a Catholic." The baptism by which we are indelibly marked is an abiding bond, and a magnetic force drawing us always toward the completeness of the conversion to which we are called. That conversion is perfected in obedience to the truth that freedom is discovered in obedience to the truth. For the Catholic, such obedience can in no way be separated from the community that St. Paul describes as "the household of God, which is the Church of the living God, the pillar and bulwark of the truth" (1 Timothy 3:15).

And so I end where I began. The question is whether Catholicism will be Catholic. The historical and sociological dynamics to which I alluded earlier have led to a serious unraveling, an unraveling gleefully celebrated and encouraged by the Catholic left. Liberal Catholicism, rightly understood, is an honorable tradition and could today be a source of renewal, but that depends upon its capacity and readiness to receive the invitation—an invitation so powerfully and persistently issued by this pontificate—to enter upon the high adventure of fidelity to the truth.

At the end of his aforementioned essay, Peter Steinfels lists five developments the Church must address in the new millennium: human sexuality, technological control over genes and minds, relations among world religions, changes in historical consciousness and cultural pluralism, and the meaning of individual freedom and democracy. Through encyclicals and other teaching documents, John Paul II has for twenty-four years, in obedience to the spirit and the letter of Vatican II, addressed each of those questions comprehensively, repeatedly, with formidable intelligence and persuasive force. But, with notable exceptions, his witness has not been received. Not by bishops, not by priests, not by catechists, not by traditionalists who think Vatican II was a mistake, and not by liberal Catholics who incessantly pit Vatican II against the living magisterium of the Church.

We very much need bishops who are teachers of the fullness of the faith. Perhaps God has given us the bishops we have in order to test our faith, but we know that the purpose of the episcopal office is not limited to providing spiritual trials, as salutary as spiritual trials may be. Above all, and this applies to all, we need a conversion to *ob-audire*—to responsive listening, to lively engagement, to trustful following, to the form of reflective faith that is obedience. The word went forth from the Second Vatican Council, and I believe in the promise of Isaiah 55 that "the word shall not return void." After more than three decades of confusion, contention, and conflicts that have long since become a bore to serious people, we are perhaps on the edge of genuinely receiving the Council and the living magisterium of which the Council is part; the living magisterium apart from which there would be no Council, apart from which the Council cannot be rightly understood. If so, the Catholicism that is flourishing now and will likely flourish in the future will be believably and vibrantly Catholic. If so, the consequences for the Christian movement in world history are inestimable. I believe this could happen. In fact, were I writing a book about this promise and possibility, I might very well borrow a title from myself and call it *The Catholic Moment*.

THANKSGIVING
AT FAIR ACRES

(From *Christianity Today*)

Virginia Stem Owens

When I was a teenager, my church youth group made an annual Christmas pilgrimage to what people then called the "old folks' home." We took small wrapped gifts, perhaps a comb and bottle of after-shave for men, handkerchiefs, and hand cream for women. Our youth leader did all the cheery talking. We only had to sing and grin. The more virtuous or socially skilled among us might shake a few claw-like hands or pat several bony shoulders. The rest of us just sang carols, crowding around the bedsides of strangers while exchanging sidelong glances to let one another know we understood this wasn't real, that we had no personal connection to all this creepy weirdness. As soon as we could, we escaped into the cold night air outside, our pent breath exploding in blasts of laughter.

I was not one of the better people. I dreaded these nursing-home excursions, and not merely because of the sensory and metaphysical assaults aging flesh inflicts on the young. Even at fifteen, I knew that we were putting on an act, performing—in all the variations of that word's meaning—our Christian duty.

For the most part, we had no idea who these deplorable figures were in their wheelchairs and sickbeds. We weren't even curious. The season demanded charity the way it demanded colored lights, and we provided it—or at least its ceremony. We sang at the nursing homes to warm ourselves with the glow of our own virtue in the same way we Texans use angel hair and tinsel icicles to work up a fake nostalgia for snowy winter landscapes.

As an adult, I made a few visits to elderly relatives or friends in nursing homes, but my next significant exposure came in Wyoming twenty-two years later. We had just moved to a new town and, having a lot of free time on my hands, I decided to volunteer at a VA hospital two afternoons a week. By then I was old enough myself to be curious about old people. A number of important people in my life were nearing eighty. I was beginning to face the fact that they might get seriously sick or even die someday. What would that be like?

From the patients, mostly veterans of World Wars I and II, I got an introductory course on amputation, lung cancer, and stroke. Wheeling patients to the radiology lab or physical therapy, I observed their gauze-wrapped stumps, nicotine-yellowed nails, colostomy bags. Most were men, and fitness had not been a concept, much less a priority, for them. They would sit on the side of their beds, wheezing with emphysema or struggling to drag a recognizable word from under the avalanche of a stroke-damaged brain. A few would talk, but most were sunk in the silence that comes either from illness or living alone too long.

When my circumstances changed and I was no longer able to volunteer at the hospital, I found I missed those afternoons pushing wheelchairs. They had introduced me to a world I now could see was not only real, but one with which I did indeed have some personal connection. Still, I was glad that none of my elderly relatives was living in such a place. To my knowledge, none ever had. Nor, I was certain, would my parents.

Stony, Regal Detachment

It's ten days till Thanksgiving when I push open the double doors to Fair Acres Nursing Facility in Huntsville, Texas. And eight months to the day since we first brought my mother here. My father and I had spent a year and a half caring for her at home as Parkinson's disease, dementia, and osteoporosis had become too severe. And my father, dealing himself with declining health, could no longer take care of her.

The first couple of months I came through the dark mahogany doors of Fair Acres, inset with etched glass, I was disgusted by the irony of the foyer, masquerading as a sedate, upscale hotel. Muted light from brass lamps fell on a silk-flower arrangement atop the cherry-wood sideboard. But the Ethan Allen attempt at elegance disappeared as soon as you passed the portal to the hallway. The understated lighting gave way to fluorescent overhead panels, the carpet to vinyl tile with foldup yellow signs warning of wet floors. During those early days, I would sail past the nurses' station, scanning to my right the bedraggled but still ambulatory crew occupying the waterproof Queen Anne chairs in the common living room.

Though the furniture is arranged to form a circle (a vain attempt to foster fellowship), no one talks to anyone else. The only human voice comes from a portable radio belonging to a resident who keeps it tuned to Christian talk shows. To my left, a ring of wheelchairs circles the nurses' station like beleaguered pioneer wagons. These are occupied by residents who generally require closer supervision—the rockers, the weepers, those who must be kept from falling out of their chairs by Lap Buddies, padded cushions the staff are careful never to call "restraints." (Certain words, like *patients,* are forbidden here; everyone is a *resident.*) A few in that circle of wheelchairs simply prefer that location to the living room, probably because there's more action at the nurses' station. There phones ring, staffers banter or complain to one another, family members stop to make inquiries or requests.

Despite the action, however, the people parked around the nurses' station, like their ambulatory counterparts in the living-room area, appear completely oblivious of one another. Their faces are as expressionless as the Easter Island monoliths. Several doze. One woman cries out monotonously, "Help me, help me." The rest stare resolutely ahead in stony, almost regal, detachment.

Only when visitors cross the rotunda do they glance up at the alien outsiders bringing in their determined, facile cheer. Their look accuses: "Don't think you're doing us any favor. You're not getting off the hook that easy."

After the first few weeks of running this daily gauntlet, I started speaking to some of the people I passed on the way to my mother's room. By then I had scoped out the ones I thought might respond. At first, however, none returned my greeting. A few looked up with a dazed frown, as if I had startled them from deep reverie. One or two, after a second's hesitation, gave me a single nod or at least met my gaze directly. I didn't blame the ones who ignored me. They had every right to their withdrawal.

Two-thirds of nursing-home residents have no regular visitors. Some never have any. People who have been abandoned develop a thick coat of defensive frost.

I eventually struck up an acquaintance with a woman I passed every day. At first she only looked up when I spoke to her. Then a few days later, she nodded. By the end of the week, she was returning my greeting. Now, as soon as she sees me, a certain expectancy suffuses her face and she lifts her hands to catch mine between them.

"Those hands is too cold," she tells me, shaking her head. "You need to warm up."

Stella weighs eighty pounds at most. Her lips sink over her toothless gums and her chin juts sharply like a bowsprit. Her left leg has been amputated at the knee, and her right foot, usually shod in a red flat, is positioned neatly on the wheelchair's single footrest. I have no idea how she lost the other leg. Maybe one day I'll feel I can ask. Something prompts me to compliment her frequently on her appearance, some special care she takes to straighten her sleeve or smooth her skirt over her lap. On special occasions like today—the Family Thanksgiving Dinner—she wears a string of red beads.

Viola, who lives on Two Hundred Hall, refuge of the more independent residents, is not planning to attend the Family Thanksgiving Dinner. Not many residents from that wing will. They are the establishment's upper crust, people who could conceivably function well at home but who, for one reason or another, have washed up on the shores of Fair Acres.

Most have physically debilitating diseases like severe diabetes or MS but remain in full control of their mental faculties. They form their own private club, playing cards in the activity room during the afternoon or visiting one another in their heavily decorated rooms.

Viola has lovely shoulder-length white hair, expertly waved in the manner of a 1940s movie star. Disabled by a bad heart, she, along with her cancer-riddled husband, moved to Fair Acres the day after they sold their home in a coastal city a hundred miles east of here. He died last week.

She tells me about it, sitting in her wheelchair, parked in the doorway of her room, careful to assure me that she was fully prepared for the loss, welcomed it, in fact, "for his sake."

She tells me my husband stopped to pray with her a few days ago. "He's such a dear." She makes a graceful, deprecating movement with her hand, brushing the front of her duster. "But really, I'm fine." Her own husband's empty bed, I notice, has already been filled with a new resident.

My husband has also made friends with Essie, another Two Hundred Hall resident, but one who, strangely enough, prefers to spend her days in the wagon train circling the nurses' station. Essie's son, she has confided to David, brought her to Huntsville after she'd had a stroke and installed her in Fair Acres. Now he never comes to see her. He apparently leaves that duty to his wife, a tall blonde who owns the health club where I swim.

Essie is a tall woman, or at least she would be if she could still stand. You can tell because her useless left leg, elevated on her wheelchair's footrest to improve circulation, juts out into the traffic lane around the nurses' station. Essie sleeps a good bit of the time, holding a washcloth to one side of her face to catch the saliva that flows from her stroke-slackened mouth. She was a schoolteacher in her former life, and her speech, slurred now as if she'd been on an all-night binge, retains its acerbic humor and no-nonsense flavor. She is already parked at a table when my father and I wheel my mother into the dining room. Her aerobic daughter-in-law sits at her side, looking slightly dazed.

Today is Family Thanksgiving Dinner at Fair Acres, though the holiday is more than a week away. In nursing-home time a week more or less does not make much difference. In any case, the abstractions of time are beyond my mother now, so I don't tell her that next week my husband

and I will be eating our "real" Thanksgiving dinner in Kansas with our daughters' families.

She's dressed in her newest dress and has smudges of blusher on her cheeks for the occasion. Unfortunately, though, the general air of excitement is already threatening to overwhelm her. Her eyes are darting about the room, her breath coming in short, shallow snatches.

Awkward Table Talk

The tables have been rearranged, end-to-end pilgrim-style, for the Thanksgiving feast, and my father and I take our places on both sides of my mother.

Across from us sit Norman, the owner of the Christian music boom box, and James, a black man in a Mister Rogers cardigan who moves with glacial stateliness to compensate for his halting, stroke-damaged gait. They maintain their usual distant reserve.

"May we join you?" I ask, making my voice bright with what I hope they will see as holiday cheer. James inclines his head in a courtly manner. Norman says, "Sure," and blinks several times in what appears to be welcome.

"Isn't this nice," I say enthusiastically, gesturing toward the centerpieces—baskets of orange, yellow, and red silk leaves, accented with stalks of dried grass and little plastic ears of corn. James nods; Norman says, "Yes, nice." My father grins encouragingly.

I take my mother's hand and, turning my overbright social tone down a notch, point out the centerpieces to her. She points instead to a large basket of rolls, slowly growing cold on the table. I butter one and give it to her.

Meanwhile, an aide is maneuvering the wheelchair of a woman with a rust-colored perm and a silk blouse into position across from my father. Her head shakes like Katharine

Hepburn's, and in one hand she clutches a washcloth with which she continually dabs at her mouth. The washcloth, I see, is to mop up saliva pushed toward the front of her mouth by her tongue that squirms compulsively, like some small burrowing animal.

I introduce our little party. Beaming, my father half rises and extends his hand across the table. The woman shakes it loosely and tells us her name, which, after several repetitions, I finally make out to be Mary. My mother nods shyly at the woman. I search for a conversational gambit that might spin some fine thread of connection, some link of sympathy between us across the table. I feel like an old-fashioned telephone operator, plugging an array of lines into a decrepit switchboard.

Mary struggles to respond with appropriate chitchat, drawing from her own store of social pleasantries. Over the kitchen clatter, I shout inanities across the table at Norman and James alternately. "Smell that? Mmm, turkey!" "What kind of pie are you going to have? Pumpkin or pecan?" "Want a roll to tide you over?"

Amid great bustle, the food is brought from the kitchen and laid out, buffet-style. By the time the director quiets everyone to say grace, my mother is listing acutely leftward like a rag doll in her chair. I make a break for the buffet table to fill a plate for her, James and Norman close behind me.

I load a plate with turkey, dressing, gravy, sweet potatoes, fruit salad, cranberry sauce—the dishes I know my mother has always liked. After cutting the turkey into bite-sized bits, I name the plate's contents, coaxing her appetite. "Take a bite of the dressing, Mother, you'll like it." She ignores me, making her way slowly but steadily through the turkey.

"Would you like another roll? I'll butter it for you."

She shakes her head and, after finishing the turkey, puts down her fork, leaving the rest of the meal untouched. The noise, I know, distracts her, the sounds a jumble she can't sort into meaning.

"Dessert?" I urge. "I think there's pumpkin pie. Or would you like cobbler?" She doesn't answer, but I get her a small piece of pumpkin pie. She ignores it, her panting turning suddenly panicky.

Through the Cracks

Telling my father to finish at his own pace, I wheel my mother back to her room. We're both relieved by the quiet that settles around us there. I press the call button for the aides to come and lift her into bed, then I sit beside her, holding her hand until she drops into a fitful sleep.

"It went well, don't you think?" I whisper to my father when he tiptoes into my mother's room.

I'm feeling that sappy self-satisfaction of a hostess who has just pulled off a successful dinner party. I'm even more pleased the next day when James for the first time returns my wave from his post on the Queen Anne loveseat, lifting his index finger and smiling tentatively, as if taking a social risk.

I regret, of course, that my mother was confused and isolated at the Thanksgiving table. I have to fight back the guilt that arises from enjoying anything she can't. And even when I sidestep the guilt, my grief for her threatens to engulf even my pleasure at everyone else's enjoyment. But the truth is, I did feel happy. And I don't think it came entirely from the smug satisfaction of knowing James and Norman had gotten a sliver of conversation along with their turkey and pumpkin pie. Or that Mary, probably a social powerhouse in her day, got to wow us once more with her classy blouse and nails.

"Pleased to meet you," people say in Texas when they're introduced. And I was glad, finally, to have met them all. I hope they were pleased as well. My own pleasure came from their having let me in through a crack in their carefully constructed indifference.

Through that crack I have caught a glimpse of the other side of the wall, the one I had fled in my teenage fear and carelessness, the side of the wall where I will live someday.

"How did the nursing home dinner go?" my daughter asked me the following week as we were recovering from the "real" Thanksgiving feast.

"You know that parable in Luke where the master sends his servant out to the highways and hedges to bring in the maimed, the halt, and the blind after the people he'd invited to the banquet don't show up?"

"Mmm . . . I think so."

"Well, that's how it was. And I got to come too."

BELIEF UNBRACKETED

A Case for the Religion Scholar to Reveal More
of Where He or She Is Coming From
    (From *Harvard Divinity Bulletin*)

Stephen Prothero

I am crazy for people who are crazy for God: people nearly as inscrutable to me as divinity, who leave wives and children to become forest-dwelling monks in Thailand, who wander naked across the belly of India in search of self-realization, who speak in tongues and take up serpents in Appalachia because the Bible says they can.

Over my living-room mantel stands a chorus of carved snake handlers, each holding a serpent aloft, each entrusting his life to God and to us a testimony. On my bookshelves stand a number of books on snake handling. The best is Dennis Covington's *Salvation on Sand Mountain* (1995), which describes the author's spiritual sojourn in southern Appalachia, including his dramatic decision to take up serpents himself. Briskly paced and elegantly written, this memoir raises all sorts of intriguing questions about religion and violence, faith and fanaticism. It ends, however, on a sour note.

After two years as "Brother Dennis," Covington picks a fight about women speaking in church—a fight he knows he is going to lose—and stomps out the door. Such endings are axiomatic in the "in and out" spiritual memoir, and I was disappointed that Covington fell into the cliché. Still, I forgave him the ungraceful exit, because the rest of the book is such a graceful introduction to the slings and arrows of hardcore faith (and because I knew he needed to get back home).

Harvard Divinity School Professor Robert Orsi is not so forgiving. In a provocative essay called "Snakes Alive: Resituating the Moral in the Study of Religion," he praises Covington for providing "a good model for engaged, interpersonal, participatory religious study," then chastises him for getting above his raisin' at the end. According to Orsi, Covington commits at the conclusion of his quest the unpardonable sin of "otherizing": of defining himself over against his subjects and then judging them to be morally inferior to himself.[1]

What Covington should have done, Orsi argues, is linger in the no-man's land between going native and going home, forever flirting not only with his subjects but also with his own identity. He should have practiced the "erotics of Religious Studies" by suspending ad infinitum his judgments, endlessly playing his own religious world against the worlds of his subjects, and otherwise refusing closure. "Religious studies is not a moralizing discipline," Orsi concludes. "It exists in the suspension of the ethical."[2]

Orsi is a brilliant theorist of religion and perhaps more than any of us (certainly more than I) he is alive to the ambiguities and complexities of religious experience, its everyday shame and violence. Still, he is saying little new here. For more than a century, scholars of religion have been distinguishing themselves from theologians by attempting to bracket questions of truth, morality, and causality—all in the name of better understanding religious phenomena. More than any other idea, Edmund Husserl's notion of bracketing, or *epochē* (from the Greek for "holding back"), has defined Religious Studies as a discipline. What do folks like me do? We enter empathetically into the worlds of religious people in an attempt to understand the believers who inhabit them. We set aside questions of cause and effect, good and bad. We check our worldviews at the door. Or, as Orsi puts it, we "enter into the otherness of religious practices in search of an understanding of their human ground."[3]

My latest book, *American Jesus: How the Son of God Became a National Icon*, is an attempt to do just that—in this case to understand the myriad images of Jesus that have inspired Americans from Thomas Jefferson to Jerry Falwell. Though, as the subtitle intimates, one burden of the book is to explain how Americans transformed their Jesus from an abstract theological sign into a concrete person and finally into a celebrity, on the whole it is an attempt at what the Dutch religionist Gerardus van der Leeuw called *Verstehen,* or empathetic understanding.

As my book has been read, reviewed, and debated, however, I have come to believe that the endless bracketing that I have always taken as my charge is viable only as long as our work exists in the splendid isolation of the Ivory Tower. In the rough and tumble of the real world, it is not possible, and likely not desirable.

※

In a review of *American Jesus* published in *The New York Times Book Review*, Michael Massing, apparently taking as a personal challenge my refusal to plump for any particular Jesus, went on a quest for "Prothero's own Jesus" and found him in the person of Jefferson's rationalist sage. In the daily *Times*, R. Scott Appleby described me as a partisan of the "religion bad, spirituality good" school. Both claims concern my personal religious beliefs—a subject the book dutifully avoids—and are plainly false. As I wrote in a letter to the *Times*, I personally find Jefferson's Jesus laughably ahistorical. And while as a historian I see the partisans of disorganized religion as key players in America's spiritual marketplace, I nonetheless consider the disdain of so many Baby Boomers for religious institutions as ungenerous at best. (Where, after all, do yoga and meditation come from? Why such disdain for the dead?)[4]

Perhaps more effectively than prying reviewers, inquiring readers draw us out, too, demanding that we serve up our expertise with a bit of judgment. Over the last few months, I have participated in dozens of media interviews about my book. Virtually every interviewer has eventually gotten around to matters of judgment. Which Jesus is your favorite? Is the proliferation of Jesuses a good or a bad thing? What would Jesus say about Buddhist and Hindu appropriations of his image? Is Jesus the Christ? Of course, some of these questions can be deflected, and I tried that for a while. But interviewers quickly grow tired of the cat-and-mouse game that is Religious Studies, and eventually so did I.

To my horror (and delight), I am now on the record against Jefferson's vision of Jesus as an enlightened sage and for representations of Jesus as a Black Moses. I have told interviewers that I am a Christian (albeit a confused one), that Mel Gibson's film *The Passion of the Christ* is 99 and 44/100ths made up, that Hindu conceptions of Jesus as an avatar are deliciously bold, and that Jesus would not drive a car (unless he lived in Los Angeles).

In other words, I have come to see the "erotics of Religious Studies" as a tease. What is the danger of divulging to our readers what we really think (however confused or provisional)? Does criticizing our subjects really do them grave harm? Are Religious Studies scholars really so powerful? Our readers so impressionable? Our subjects so weak?

In all this handwringing about bracketing beliefs and suspending the ethical, I find more than a trace of condescension toward readers and subjects alike. In *Salvation on Sand Mountain,* a preacher named Punkin Brown bears the brunt of Covington's ire. In "Snakes Alive," Orsi rushes with bodhisattva resolve to Brown's rescue, and to the aid of Covington's readers (who presumably have been horribly betrayed by the author's moral provocation). I do not know for sure, but I rather doubt that Punkin Brown was undone by the feminist rantings of a scribbling outlander, or that the book's readers are powerless to resist Covington's theologizing.

When I was in college, a group of students gathered regularly a bit after midnight and argued, often for hours, about politics, economics, and religion. It was an eclectic crew. We had Marxists, liberals, conservatives, an atheist, a Jew, a born-again Christian, and a conservative and a liberal Catholic. We went at one another, no holds barred, consigning our friends to heaven and hell, calling Christianity (Marxism as well) an opiate of the masses, and otherwise making all manner of outrageous judgments about the world and ourselves. As far as I know, none of us was hurt by any of the provocation. And I learned more about myself (and real friendship) in those sessions than I did in all my college courses combined.

✶

At points in "Snakes Alive," Orsi seems to describe Religious Studies as an enterprise of just this sort of provocation: You venture into the dangerous border zone "between one's own moral universe and the moral world of the other" and come out a changed person. But when the contest is engaged and push comes to shove, Orsi becomes gun-shy. For him, Covington's principled assertion of women's rights "amounts to a refusal to engage his real subject." I could not disagree more. To tiptoe around the tough issues is to turn away. To tackle them head-on is true engagement.

One of my college friends, David L. Chappell (the village atheist in our early morning debates), is now a history professor at the University of Arkansas. His most recent book, *A Stone of Hope: Prophetic Religion and the Death of Jim Crow* (2004), is a masterly study of the powerful role religion played in the civil rights movement.[5] It is also a timely rebuke to the timidity of Religious Studies, and of my own reticence to move beyond bracketing to moral inquiry. In it, Chappell proceeds with all the subtlety of a battering ram (or a prophet), blasting black nationalist interpreters of the Rev. Dr. Martin Luther King Jr. as anti-intellectuals, sneering at the hokum of the philosophical/theological school of Personalism, and castigating King and other civil rights saints for their intellectual inconsistencies.

While reading this book, I kept flashing back to a very different volume: *Salvation and Suicide: An Interpretation of Jim Jones, the Peoples Temple, and Jonestown* (1988) by David Chidester, a professor at the University of Cape Town. I had been at college only a few weeks when Jim Jones and more than nine hundred of his followers perished in a mass suicide-murder in Guyana in November 1978. Night after night, I was riveted to the radio, taking in Jones's haunting sermons. In retrospect, these broadcasts may have been the catalyst that diverted me from astrophysics (my major at the time) to American religious history. I wanted to know why Jonestown happened. I wanted explanations.

A classic example of Orsi's "erotic methodology," *Salvation and Suicide* dances around these concerns with a smile and a swagger, making it not only one of the most brilliant books in the field but also one of the most perverse. Chidester proudly refuses "causal explanations," offering instead a "religiohistorical interpretation" that seeks to understand empathetically what turned Jonestown into a "meaningful human enterprise." After invoking his method of "temporarily" suspending value judgments, he writes, "I stress the word *temporarily* here because after the strategy of *epochē* has been exercised, and the phenomenon we are exploring has appeared in as much clarity as we can bring to it, we can always go on (or back) to making moral judgments." Yet he never goes on, or back. True to his training (and my own), he refuses to moralize, except about the meaningfulness of Jonestown for its participants.[6]

This is what Religious Studies is all about. And if Orsi is right that excessive moralizing is the discipline's ever-present danger, then we should have more of it. Still, I can't help thinking that our problem is not a surfeit of judgment but a dearth—that the danger is not in silencing our Punkin Browns but silencing ourselves. Revolutions never seem to be able to stop at drawing blood; inevitably they end up flaying corpses. And here Orsi seems to be doing battle not so much with his colleagues today as with ghosts of religionists past.

Since Jonestown, religion has shown its dark side repeatedly—with Heaven's Gate, at Waco, and on 9/11. In each case, we Religious Studies scholars have been largely irrelevant to the public debates. True, we drew out the parallels between the Heaven's Gate Website and medieval Daoist immortality texts. But we could not explain what produced the worst mass suicide on American soil. No surprise, then, that radio and television producers turned instead to self-styled "cult experts" to explain what happened when Heaven's Gate swung shut. And to experts on the Middle East rather than Islamicists when it came to parsing Islam as "a religion of peace."

Here's a thought: Perhaps it is time to stop "otherizing" ourselves. In homage to Husserl, Orsi, Chidester, and all the ghosts of Religious Studies past, let us continue to suspend the ethical and understand with empathy. Let us delight in difference and tear down the barriers between ourselves and our subjects. But then also tear down this barrier: the barrier against our own judgments. If we really want to resuscitate religion as a moral enterprise, make bracketing a temporary strategy rather than an eternal imperative. Before you leave southern Appalachia, tell Punkin Brown what you think of him. He can take it (or leave it). So can our readers. Maybe Religious Studies (and I) can too.

Notes

1. Robert Orsi, "Snakes Alive: Resituating the Moral in the Study of Religion," in Elizabeth A. Castelli and Rosamond C. Rodman, *Women, Gender, Religion: A Reader* (New York: Palgrave, 2001), pp. 99, 112. My thanks to Julie Byrne of Texas Christian University for drawing this essay to my attention.
2. Orsi, "Snakes Alive," pp. 117, 115.
3. Orsi, "Snakes Alive," p. 106.
4. Michael Massing, "America's Favorite Philosopher," *The New York Times Book Review* (December 28, 2003), p. 7; R. Scott Appleby, "When They Say Jesus, Which Jesus Do They Mean?" *The New York Times* (January 8, 2004), p. E9; Stephen Prothero, letter to the editor, *The New York Times* (January 18, 2004).

5. David L. Chappell, *A Stone of Hope: Prophetic Religion and the Death of Jim Crow* (Chapel Hill: University of North Carolina Press, 2004).

6. Orsi, "Snakes Alive," p. 115; David Chidester, *Salvation and Suicide: An Interpretation of Jim Jones, the Peoples Temple, and Jonestown* (Bloomington: Indiana University Press, 1988), pp. xv, xii, 46, xiv.

MY AFRICA PROBLEM . . . AND OURS

(From *The New Pantagruel*)

Gideon Strauss

Africa makes a mockery of what we say, at least what I say, about equality and questions our pieties and our commitments because there's no way to look at what's happening over there and its effect on all of us and conclude that we actually consider Africans as our equals before God. There is no chance.
—BONO OF U2, COMMENCEMENT ADDRESS AT THE
  UNIVERSITY OF PENNSYLVANIA, MAY 17, 2004.

I arrived in Canada on January 1, 1998, having flown as far from Johannesburg in South Africa as it is possible to fly before turning back around the curve of the globe. I came to Canada because I was broken and needed a break, but the way in which I was broken was as nothing compared to those whom I had spoken on behalf of in the previous two years.

I had worked for the South African Truth and Reconciliation Commission, chaired by a saint with the foibles of a saint, Desmond Tutu. The Arch, as we all called him, would hug us as we came out of our booths at the end of the day, and once, in a red-dirt town where an angry mob danced their vengeful anguish, surging hurricane-like around the hall in which the hearings were being held, he prayed through the noon hour in my booth, seeking and finding guidance to bring peace—or at least calm—to the situation. My job was not a lofty one; I was not a commissioner or a lawyer or an investigator; I was a simultaneous interpreter.

We interpreters were a small but dedicated crew. We bounced three or four languages among one another to enable an audience to hear the testimony of a survivor or a perpetrator of gross human rights violations—abduction, torture, murder—in their own language within two to four seconds after it was spoken in the language of the witness or applicant for amnesty. Many of us drank hard; some of us found harder ways of numbing the pain and horror we spoke every day. For me the worst was the phone calls late at night between me in my hotel room and my young wife at home, when, exhausted—she after a day in the valley of the shadow of the diapers and I after a day of a woman telling of relentless violation or a man telling of testicles and bare electric wire or a mother telling of the sweaters of her infants scarlet with gunshot or a father telling of finding only a scrap of skin after three days of looking in the place where a mine shredded his son—we would curse and slam down the phone, too tired to listen and too worn out to care.

When I came to Canada I thought I would be going back. Soon. Maybe after four or five years, with another academic degree certifying me for the ministry of word and sacrament in my home church. Eighteen months later the strange configuration of calling and debt moved me into the work I do now with delight and an assurance that it is what I should be doing. Africa faded, slowly. Asked some months later if I would not help found a leadership school back in South Africa, I collapsed into a profound vocational crisis—perhaps the most profound yet. What are my duties to Africa? Should I abandon the work I do here in North America—holy work, as far as I can tell—and turn to the cries of the beloved country? Should I return with my wife and young daughters to a country that at the time had the highest incidence of rape as reported to the police of any Interpol member country?

My Africa problem is not whether there is something wrong with Africa, or whether something should be done about it if there is. Both reliable research and my own direct experience assure me that something is indeed very wrong with Africa, and I have no doubt that something should be done about it. My problem has to do with what should be done, and by whom. More particularly, what is my own personal responsibility toward Africa, and how does that responsibility weigh up against my other responsibilities?

I grew up in an all-white residential neighborhood where I was told during my childhood that black people could only live in the outbuildings if they had an employment document as a house servant or a gardener, and that a sunset-to-sunrise curfew for black people kept our streets safe. I was told that people in my neighborhood enjoyed a quality of life unequaled in the world, except perhaps in Sweden. Health care was excellent by the standards of the time. The streets were paved, and regular watering kept the parks green and filled with flowers, even though our city was on the edge of an arid semi-desert. Schools did a fairly good job, and music lessons—if you wanted them—were virtually free, because they were offered as a normal, albeit optional, part of the education system. (I learned to play the viola, poorly.)

In my teens, after my cataclysmic conversion to biblical Christianity (as distinct from the racist pseudo-Christian heresy of my childhood and the Buddhism Lite of my early teens), I became involved with an avowedly apolitical youth evangelism group in my home town that for all its intended denial of politics nonetheless had an enormous political influence on me and my friends. This group was the only interracial Christian youth group we could find in the city, and its evangelistic outreaches and youth camps brought me face-to-face with people of my own age who lived in very different circumstances from my own.

My black teen friends lived not ten minutes by car from where I lived. Their neighborhood had no electricity and only cold running water made available at public water taps, each shared by four residential blocks. Their streets were not paved, and night waste was removed by a truck that came by every few days. The schools were poorly supplied with books and hardly supplied with anything else. As one of the architects of this racially based political system—Hendrik Verwoerd—had explained some years before I was born:

> When I have control of Native education I will reform it so that Natives will be taught from childhood to realize that equality with Europeans is not for them. . . . People who believe in equality are not desirable teachers for Natives. When my Department controls Native education it will know for what class of higher education a Native is fitted, and whether he will have a chance in life to use his knowledge.

Many of my black friends, but especially their parents, managed to strain considerable dignity and a simple beauty of life out of the sordid circumstances into which they had been pressed. But to my young eyes the inequality between them and us was obvious, and obviously a grave injustice.

I remember discovering—with shock that turned into deep conviction—the prophecy of Isaiah 58.

> . . . day after day they seek me out; they seem eager
> to know my ways, as if they were a nation that does

what is right and has not forsaken the commands of its God. They ask me for just decisions and seem eager for God to come near them. . . . Is this the kind of fast I have chosen, only a day for a man to humble himself? . . . Is not this the kind of fasting I have chosen: to loose the chains of injustice and untie the cords of the yoke, to set the oppressed free and break every yoke?

My friends and I poured ourselves into the resistance against the apartheid regime. Our involvement in that resistance was no great shakes—we were very young, we had no idea what we were doing, and our connections into the existing resistance movements were very weak—but it was enough to get us into tepid water. I was invited to go and discuss my activities with the security police a few times, where it became clear that they had reliable information from one of my good friends, and my parents were reminded by someone or other that my activities might have negative repercussions for their careers. But nothing like the hot water that the black teens in our circle endured: ninety-day detentions without trial, beatings with sand-filled nylon-stoking tubes, disappearances, and as we discovered years later, worse.

We thought we would spend our lives on resistance against a racist tyranny. We struggled terrifically to understand the connection between our deepest loves (for God, for one another) and our duties as citizens. We read—Ron Sider and John Howard Yoder, at first; later Francis Schaeffer and Bob Goudzwaard; eventually Herman Dooyeweerd, Abraham Kuyper, John Calvin, and Augustine of Hippo. We argued. We prayed. At first we became pacifists and therefore understood our political duties to demand nonviolence. I served three–and-a-half years of a six-year community service assignment as a religious objector against military conscription. Later, toward the end of the 1980s, some of us turned to Just War doctrine and tried to figure out an understanding of just resistance against a tyrant. We never got very far theoretically, but we persuaded ourselves that the ever more vigorous violent oppression practiced by the then Botha government demanded from us as Christians armed resistance.

We never got around to doing something about that conviction, because just as we stopped being pacifists the new De Klerk government announced that it would release all political prisoners, including Nelson Mandela, unban all banned political movements, and begin a process of negotiation toward a democratic South Africa. That all happened what is now almost half my life ago, but it remains perhaps the most decisive historical event to have a direct impact on my life. Suddenly I had no idea what my life was supposed to be about. If I was not to expend my life in the struggle against apartheid, then into what would I invest myself?

I floundered. I wrote an M.A. dissertation (on Christian philosophy and the transformation of African culture) and a Ph.D. thesis (titled "The Ethics of Public Welfare") in an effort to try to figure out what I should do in the aftermath of apartheid. I joined political movements, and with a friend, Mark Manley, I tried to put together a network of evangelical Christians active in postapartheid South Africa. I worked on language policy and the constitutional rights of language groups with another friend, Theo du Plessis. I worked for the Truth and Reconciliation Commission, and I went slightly crazy. But I still had no idea what to do with my life now that I had nothing big and evil and obvious to be against.

The first democratic elections of 1994 were astonishing, with the nation teetering at the edge of the abyss of civil war (not white versus black, but something complex that could be oversimplified into Zulu versus Xhoza) and then pulling back—a peaceful result partly due to nationwide prayer, it seemed to many of us. Standing for hours in the long line snaking into a school hall to cast our ballots next to people of all tongues and races was perhaps the highest point in my political life. South Africa's victory in the 1995 Rugby World Cup tournament provoked a surge of shared patriotism that drew the people of the country together into a moment of common celebration the likes of which have not been seen before, or since.

But postapartheid South Africa was a disappointment. Along with my other work, I spent a few days every month interpreting for the provincial parliament of what was once known as the Orange Free State province. It was a dismal affair. The plenary sessions were displays of the small-minded mediocrity of the provincial politicians of all parties. The committee sessions were displays of venality and petty power games. A tinge of backlash racism marked the operations of the new provincial government. A friend of mine, the finest development economist in the province and a long-time opponent of apartheid, raised funding internationally for the research and design of an economic development approach in the province, but because he was white the provincial government mocked and ignored the potential of his contribution. Hints of corruption and self-enrichment were everywhere—the new provincial cabinet members drove shiny Mercedes Benzes or BMWs, while the common people sank into ever greater poverty. Many of my most idealistic friends sank, not into poverty, but into a sour and depressed cynicism and pessimism about the future of the beloved country.

The political efforts in which I involved myself were bearing little or no fruit. Most Christians involved in politics did not want to think christianly about their political duties, preferring instead a simplistic para-marxism or a vulgar nationalism. Those Christians who were willing to think christianly about their politics tended to fall for a triumphalistic imported version of the politics of the American religious right—but since their numbers were small, their efforts were ineffectual. Networking Christians who were biblically thoughtful about political life in South Africa in the mid-1990s foundered on the rocks of nonbiblical ideology, simplistic biblicism, and a general lack of interest.

Increasingly I became persuaded that South African Christians were not ready for political responsibility because we lacked a thoroughly Christian understanding, not just of politics, but of culture in general. The ground in which my friends and I were trying to sow the seeds of Christian political action lacked compost and had not been plowed over. For a Christian politics to flourish in South Africa, Christian political activists needed to take a step back. The soil needed to be tilled, and compost needed to be worked into the fields. The most important political work in South Africa, I came to believe, was that of proclaiming the gospel. The proclamation of the gospel of the creation and redemption of all things in Christ was needed before Christian political action could become viable.

With that in mind I began to consider the ministry of Word and sacraments in my home denomination, then the Presbyterian Church of Southern Africa. If a Christian politics in South Africa was for the time being impossible—or at least limited to education—then perhaps my calling was to do the work of preparing Christians for a Christian politics in the generations to come? Perhaps I could preach the Word and serve the sacraments in ways that would help cultivate discernment and conviction with regard to the duties of citizenship, Biblically understood?

Things did not turn out that way. I spent eighteen months in Vancouver, British Columbia, thinking that I was preparing for the Presbyterian ministry in South Africa. Our family went through its own little posttraumatic stress episode, whacked on top of consumer culture shock of the first degree, ameliorated by living in one of the most beautiful cities in the world (ah, the float planes drifting in over the bay against a gilt and russet sunset) and being embraced by Regent College, which turned out to serve us more as a therapeutic community than as a place of professional advancement. And then I was offered work with the two organizations in which I still find myself following the call of God today. We left Vancouver for Toronto, and with that decided that if we were to return to live and work in Africa, it would be after our children went to college, if ever.

But is this the right thing to do? What Would Bono Do? Consider Africa today. While South Africa has not collapsed into failed statehood, as many people feared, it is one of the most criminally violent places in the world. In contrast, the neighboring Botswana has relatively little crime—but it suffers from one of the highest rates of HIV infection in the world. Zimbabwe is governed by a caricature dictator whose comic ridiculousness is rivaled only by his malevolence. Further up, in the Sudan, another genocide looms, perhaps on the same scale as that achieved in Rwanda. Everywhere Africa is plagued by disease, poverty, crime, and political situations that seem to allow a choice only between tyranny and anarchy. And yet this is a continent where people continue to choose the Christian faith over their native paganisms, where churches thrive and grow, where despite an ecstatic strain of piety among the mass of people, church leaders seem to have a bent for sound doctrine. Ever so slowly—as at the outer fringes of the Roman Empire from the fifth century to the twelfth century—

Christianity seems to be working itself into the soil of African culture. The Christian transformation of African culture seems likely to be a five-hundred-year project. What can I do to help it along?

Writing this meandering memoir has brought me no closer to a personal vocational answer than the nights of prayer and tears of a few years ago. The comfort of my present sense of calling has never been so cozy that it requires an exercise of this kind to be shaken. A few weeks ago I sat next to a philosopher and a new friend, who quietly but passionately asked me, "But how can you be here and not there?" For now my retort is, that is not only my problem. It is ours.

TO SKELLIG MICHAEL, MONASTERY IN THE SKY

(From *Books & Culture*)

Daniel Taylor

A saint is one who exaggerates what the world neglects.
—G. K. CHESTERTON

Skellig Michael is a seven-hundred-foot-high pinnacle of water-and-wind-worn rock that rises like Excalibur out of the Atlantic waves off the southwest coast of Ireland. If you have ever been there, you do not need it described; if you have not been, no description is adequate. The same is true of that part of reality called the sacred.

I make my reluctant pilgrimage to Skellig Michael in near total ignorance, based solely on three sentences in a guidebook. I expect the usual visitor center and gift shop. Instead, the voice of the fisherman's wife on the phone says, "Be at the Portmagee pier at ten-thirty tomorrow morning. If the weather is good enough, my husband will be there in his boat to pick you up." The weather the next day is unusually fine, and down the inlet we watch him chug, my son Nate and I, his only passengers for the day.

We hop on board and start out toward the sea. The engine of the fishing boat is loud enough to make talking difficult, and it fills the air with diesel fumes. It's just under an hour out to Skellig Michael, depending on your boat and the conditions. You don't see the island when you start out from the harbor, but soon you are passing looming Bray's

Head and there it is on the horizon, the first step into the Atlantic. Tiny at first, it's shrouded today in a thin white haze. It looks mystical—in part because I expect it to look mystical. I think of Avalon, the island to which King Arthur was carried on the barge of singing women, there to recover from his wounds and, someday, return again to a new Camelot. Will my own wounds be soothed today?

Approaching Skellig Michael from the north, we are following a path taken so many centuries ago by a boatload of monks looking for a place to battle the flesh and the devil. They saw themselves as engaged in a war whose object was to be like Christ—that is, to be more like what they were created to be. They saw themselves as spiritual warriors. Their aim, however, was not to kill someone else, but to destroy false selves, to shed counterfeit versions of their own life, so that they might help bring into reality the kingdom of the High King of Heaven.

As is so often the case in fable and tale, we have a harbinger that we are approaching a special place. About halfway out, I spot a dart of color winging past the boat at frantic speed. It is a puffin, that compact burst of bird and bill that spends the majority of its life in air and water, touching the land only in obscure places to devote a short time to the birth, feeding, and protection of a puffin chick.

Puffins come to Skellig Michael at the same time we had come to England, in late March, their bills in the process of changing color from the dull yellow of winter to the bright red, blue, and yellow of summer. It is May now and they have taken over Skellig rabbit holes and other burrows. But they have approached Skellig Michael cautiously, as I am doing. When the puffins first arrive from unmarked journeys in the North Atlantic, they keep their distance from the island, floating for days in the sea, within sight, but not venturing on the island itself.

I understand their caution. If Skellig Michael is, as they say, a sacred place, then I'm not sure I want to be there. I remember what happened to the poor sap who tried to steady the Ark of the Covenant when it was falling off the wagon. Iona and Lindisfarne have small numbers of people living safely on them today, undoubtedly a few no better than I am. But Skellig Michael is now alone again, severe and solitary, not a place you'd want to spend the night. Perhaps it does not suffer tourists gladly.

✼

Skellig Michael, like two other famous monastic islands I have visited in years past, is named for the archangel, who reputedly came to Ireland to help Patrick with the snakes and the demons. But that name came later. When that first boat load of monks approached, it was only a skeilic—a stone island—one of many islands off the west coast of Ireland. Why did they choose this one? What seemed promising? What made them hopeful? What told them that God was better to be found or served here than at the place they came from?

Perhaps they liked that it points to the sky. Skellig Michael is 714 feet of stony verticality, a natural Gothic cathedral with narrow spikes of eroded rock decorating it like gargoyles. It has twin peaks, one at each end, like the fingertips of two parted hands lifted to heaven. Making no compromise with horizontal reality, it thrusts straight up from the sea floor to the clouds. Any living thing that dares to ride its audacious breaching of the sea will have to hold on for dear life.

Fittingly, there is no place for our boat to tie up. Skellig Michael is little more accessible now than it was fourteen-hundred years ago when the monks arrived. Nate and I jump off the boat onto a concrete platform that has been stuck like a limpet to the base of a cliff—on an island that is all cliffs. The captain backs the boat away, telling us he will wait out in the ocean until he sees we have returned to the platform. I find myself hoping he is a vigilant and reliable man.

We walk a few minutes on a narrow nineteenth-century concrete path built to service a lighthouse that once provided the only human beings on Skellig Michael but now is fully automated. The path circles around near the base of the island toward and intersects some medieval steps that will take us higher.

Actually there are three ancient pathways to the top of Skellig Michael. An eastern ascent begins near the landing platform and another path starts out from Blue Cove on the northern side of the island. Today there are only a handful of days a year during which a boat could successfully approach the northern steps, part of the evidence that climatic conditions were different in the first few centuries of monastic life than they are today.

Three paths up the mountain. It reminds me of the favorite metaphor of religious universalists. "There are many paths up the mountain," they say, suggesting that most all quests for the spiritual are equally valid. It is a tempting view, one that certainly fits nicely with our modern let's get along, affirm everybody, who-are-you-to-say mood.

But the metaphor takes a mysterious turn on Skellig Michael. In addition to the southern ascent, there are also on the south side fourteen steps carved into solid stone that begin in the middle of nowhere in particular and lead further on to more nowhere. They do not start at the sea nor do they end in the heights. They are simply there, testimony to an unfulfilled idea—begun in hope, buttressed with sweat, but left hanging, in process and in stone.

No, I do not believe that all paths lead to the top of the mountain. Some lead off cliffs. Some rise promisingly for a ways but then descend back to the base. And some, like the fourteen Skellig steps, lead nowhere at all.

Where, I wonder, is my own path leading?

⚑

The lighthouse road intersects in a few hundred yards with the southern ascent. I am glad for it. Here, finally, is the real thing, the authentic stuff, the guidebook-promised tangible evidence of ancient spirituality. I am thankful for the steps—until I start to climb them.

I let Nate go first. No use standing in the way of eager youth. The first fifty are a delight. I study each one, trying to picture the monk who dug with maddox into the side of the cliff and the no less than two monks who would have been necessary to wrestle the thick stone slab into place.

The next fifty are also no problem for this now travel-hardened pilgrim. If after still fifty more steps I am now breathing a bit heavily, what of it? Pilgrimage is supposed to include discomfort; besides, the view is growing more spectacular with every step.

And so fifty more steps, and then another fifty.

Have you ever noticed how irrelevant spectacular scenery is to a hiker in pain? How the scope of the world narrows to the tips of your shoes and the few feet of ground immediately in front of you? It is the same with spiritual climbing. The books and brochures promise mountaintop vistas, closeness to God, serenity and peace; they don't mention that getting there, if one ever does, is a lot like a death march.

But what are another fifty steps among pilgrims? Nate is patient with me, stopping whenever he sees me staring too closely at the steep steps just a few inches from my bowed and bobbing head. So that makes, what, three hundred steps?

It is good that I don't know at this point what I will learn later. There are some twenty-three-hundred steps on Skellig Michael, not counting the lighthouse road. I have only climbed a bit over ten percent of them and already I have forgotten why I came. I have forgotten everything I have read and seen in the last six weeks. I do not recall Columba or Aidan or Cuthbert or hills where angels came down. I know only that my thighs are burning and I am again in danger of feeling sorry for myself.

Does the spiritual have a snowball's chance in hell as long as we are tethered to these bodies? I know I shouldn't use a word like tethered. I know I am supposed to celebrate the God-created physicality of things—that's what all the balanced people tell me, the Celtic saints included. But the body is a nuisance sometimes. It is so needy and whiney and insistent on getting what it wants. It is the perennial two-year-old child of our existence. And so I sit for a while and rest.

The rest does me good. The sun is warm and the breeze cool—these are physical too. I feel lucky to be here, a place I hadn't even heard of a year before. I feel lucky to be here with Nate. And I am luckier than I know. There may indeed be twenty-three-hundred steps on Skellig Michael, but only six hundred are on this southern ascent. I am halfway there—though at this point I don't know where there is.

Another few hundred steps take us to Christ's Saddle, the only open patch of ground on the island, and the place I assume I am climbing to. Christ's Saddle, so named by the monks, is a small scrap of ground (less than half an acre it appears to me, though I am no good at estimating such things) that lies between the two peaks of Skellig Michael, which tower over it on either side.

It would be too generous to call it level; there is no such thing on the island. It is more of a hump—a saddle.

Walk a few dozen yards across to the north side and you find yourself staring down at birds flying beneath you, the sea acting as a green backdrop five hundred feet below. It's disorienting to be looking down at flying birds, and I back away from the deadly attraction-repulsion of great heights.

Nate and I walk toward South Peak, climbing a few yards up its base until the grass runs out and further climbing seems impossible. We sit in the warm sun and look at the small place where I imagine the monks working this bit of soil, which some think was brought here from the mainland, basket by basket, by the monks themselves. After this tiring ascent I have both great admiration for the successive groups of twelve or so men who lived here for six hundred years—and great questions about their sanity.

After visiting in 1910, George Bernard Shaw called Skellig Michael "an incredible, impossible, mad place. I tell you the thing does not belong to any world that you and I have lived and worked in; it is part of our dream world." I understand what Shaw is saying, but the sweat running down my back is not a dream. And it was real sweat for those monks who scampered up and down the cliffs, snatching eggs from bird nests on rocky ledges high above the sea. And it was real sweat when they were killing seals for meat and skins to trade with passing sailors for fishing hooks and staples, and when they were growing small patches of grain in this little bit of soil hundreds of feet in the air between the two peaks of the island. It is important to remember the reality of that sweat, because we must keep these men like us if they are to do us any good.

I am also feeling real hunger at the moment. Nate had refused breakfast this morning because he had decided to fast for the day. I was unprepared for it but not surprised. My kids often do in practice the things I heartily support in theory. Given Nate's plan to fast, my uneaten bowl of cereal before me had seemed suddenly gluttonous. I announced I would be happy to join him, and now my stomach was asking whether I hadn't been a bit impulsive.

I look out over the sea and spot our boat, waiting patiently, as promised, for us to have our pilgrim experience. The sight of it is comforting, assuring me of the needed escape when I've had enough of the sacred.

It is not hard, however, to picture another time and another boat whose sighting would have brought a gasp and a sick feeling in the stomach—a Viking boat. Viking raiders first struck an Irish monastery in 795, two years after their initial attack on the monastery at Lindisfarne in northern England. It was just a matter of time before they found the little community of monks sitting atop this isolated rock off the coast of Kerry.

The Irish called them Finngaill—the fair foreigners. They were the stateless terrorists of their day, which is exactly how John Henry Newman described them: "They ravaged far and wide at will, and no retaliation on them was possible, for these pirates . . . had not a yard of territory, a town, or a fort, no property but their vessels, no subjects but their crews."

They traveled on the superhighways of the time—the open seas. Their dragon-headed longboats could be up to 130 feet in length and carry hundreds of men, and could land almost anywhere. More often they were smaller, with a typical crew of thirty to forty, but these smaller craft could attack in fleets of dozens.

Or alone. It would not have taken a fleet to pillage Skellig Michael. One ship could appear on the horizon. It would not have had to be in a hurry. Where were the monks to go? Iona, though small, is filled with rocky hills and crags that could provide some protection. Lindisfarne, though open and flat, is very near the mainland, to which the monks could flee. But Skellig Michael is the equivalent of a modern-day office tower. If death is approaching from below, there is nothing to do but wait or jump.

The Skellig Michael monastery, unlike others, was not a rich morsel for the Vikings. Barely a crumb. It would have had a minimum of the liturgical instruments made of precious metals, and sometimes jewels, that the Vikings were looking for. But it was a place to pillage, and pillaging was their call.

The first recorded Viking attack on Skellig Michael took place in 812. They had a habit of coming back, checking in every few years on places they had raided before to see what restocking might have gone on. They paid another visit to Skellig Michael in 823 and this time took the abbot with them. The Annals of Innisfallen does not tell us much, but enough to give an insight into Viking cruelty: "Scelec was plundered by the heathens and Etgal was carried off into captivity, and he died of hunger on their hands." A man hardened by a lifetime of fasting does not starve quickly. But the Vikings apparently were in no hurry.

The Annals calls them "heathens." That is not an acceptable word today. We are told it is intolerant to use any word that suggests that one way up the mountain is superior to another. One man's heathenism is another man's indigenous religion. But as I sit now next to South Peak on Christ's Saddle, imagining a Viking boat sailing patiently but inexorably toward me, laughter and taunts coming over the water, mixing with the cry of birds, I am not inclined to imagine that I am seeing the approach of fellow spiritual seekers.

The Vikings came again in 833 and 839. It must have changed the way the monks of Skellig Michael perceived their place in the world. They had come there in imitation of the Desert Fathers of the fourth century, whom Irish

Christians greatly admired. Early Christians went to the deserts of Egypt and elsewhere for many reasons, but primarily to escape everything that would distract them from their dance with God.

Most of those distractions were embodied in civilization—in cities and empires, in getting and spending, in making and selling, in marrying and childrearing, in all the endless activities and contacts entailed in living with others. All these horizontal demands were seen as the enemy of the main purpose of our creation—to know and be in right relationship with the God who made us. The desert was attractive to these earliest of Christians, as Thomas Merton has pointed out, precisely because there was nothing there. It was an empty space—empty of people, governments, markets, and trivial demands—waiting to be filled with spiritual significance.

We are quite sure today that these people were, to be polite, misguided, possibly disturbed. Some sat for years on tall pillars, some starved themselves into vision-filled stupors, some competed with each other to win triathlons of the soul.

We moderns think they were deluded, but the Irish thought they were grand. They lamented that they had no deserts of their own to retreat to, so they settled for the wooded deserts of the forests, and the stony deserts of the anchorage, and the blue-green deserts of the sea.

When the first monks saw Skellig Michael, they saw a desert—a place away. Sitting in their cells at six hundred feet they were higher and more isolated even than Simon Stylites on his sixty-foot pillar. They were free to do what was important in life.

For two hundred years that dearly loved isolation must have seemed almost complete. They surely had some regular contact with the mainland for they would have needed to be supplied bread for communion. And they had the occasional visitor or new member. But contact with the rest of the world was infrequent and at their own choosing.

The Viking raids changed all that. The Irish desert had been violated, and could be again at any time. The monks likely did not fear death from the fair foreigners. They feared violation of their sacred space and their sacred routine. It was no longer possible to leave the world. The world had come to them—bearing swords.

I say they did not fear death from the Vikings, but of course that is true only in the abstract. A monk, watching from Christ's Saddle as a group of axe-wielding, blood-seeking Vikings climbed up the very steps Nate and I had climbed, could not have helped but be afraid. No amount of piety and prioritized thinking can keep the heart from racing in the face of someone wanting to put a hatchet in your forehead.

But at the same time that their adrenaline was surging, they were likely to be more concerned that they die well. As Geoffrey Moorhouse has put it, "If they were to die, they hoped to do so fully recognised for what they were." He imagines them gathering to say the Lord's Prayer after they first see the Viking ship, and then scattering to hide what few holy objects they possess among the rocks.

I am both intrigued and convicted by the phrase "fully recognised for what they were." We live in a culture in which serious religious faith is slightly embarrassing. Faith is seen as possibly a value—something hoped for—and not as a fact—something known. It is benign or even useful for food drives and homeless shelters, but ugly and even dangerous when it publicly asserts its claims as truth. Therefore it is asked to stay private, to speak only when spoken to, to stay in the corner and mind its very limited business.

The Celtic Christians could not have imagined such a thing. All of life was to be organized in light of spiritual realities. There was not a separate truth for monks and for kings, and when kings needed correcting, they were corrected. In the meantime, daily life was an ordered rhythm of worship, work, and study—all as an offering to God. That at least was the intent, though of course human nature often exacted its due.

I am more a modern man than a Celtic Christian in this regard. I want to be polite. I want to get along. When alone in a restaurant, I do not bow my head over meals. I do not cite the Bible in making arguments to people who put little value in it. I do not want anyone organizing prayer in public schools. I do not want my political leaders invoking God as the source of their every policy. And, in the same spirit, I try not to roll my eyes when my colleagues start talking about going to psychics or of prosperity energy fields in their homes.

But I wonder if I am so eager to fit in that I am afraid to be "fully recognised" for what I am. Would I have knelt in prayer as that out-of-breath Viking raised his axe over me on Christ's Saddle, or might I have offered to show him where the treasures were hidden in hopes of staying alive a bit longer? More to the point, how willing am I to organize my own life and actions and relationships around those spiritual truths that I claim should define every life? How eager am I to be fully recognized?

Some tell us—and have been for two hundred years— that Christianity is dying, hopelessly outdated, destined to be dug up and puzzled over by distant anthropologists as we do now with Easter Island statues. Others say no, the spiritual is again reasserting itself, as it always will, and it is militant secularism that has had its brief moment in the sun.

Sitting on Skellig Michael, I do not particularly care whether the Vikings or the monks are presently in the ascendancy. I have never placed my bets based on the odds or opinion polls. I feel the pagan instincts of my own life, but also hear the one who stands at the door and knocks. I will make my choices, like the good, individualistic westerner that I am, based on the inclinations of my own heart and the cogitations of my mind—to the extent possible given the vagaries of my will.

✘

I did not know what to expect on Skellig Michael, and I am more than pleased at what I've found. After the sea journey and hundreds of steps, I feel I have earned the exhilaration of this view and the satisfaction of imagining monks living and working and worshiping on this bit of holy ground floating in the clouds.

But as usual I am settling for too little. As I consider how long I should sit here with Nate before we head back down, I spot what I should have seen immediately after reaching Christ's Saddle. There, across the way, running up the side of and disappearing behind the north peak, is another set of steps.

I will admit to having mixed feelings about this discovery. I had thought I had arrived. I had done my climb, with the required pilgrimage pain, and had every reason to be satisfied with myself and with what I was experiencing. The views from Christ's Saddle were mind-numbing, the imaginative possibilities rich. Why did there need to be more?

Why in fact does there always seem to be more in the spiritual quest? Why does every level of discipline, of service, of intimacy with God seem inadequate? Why do our spiritual guides—living and dead—always call us to go further? Why does our goal always move, mirage-like, just beyond reach?

I find myself too easily satisfied. I am happy enough simply to be on the team. I have no great desire to be a star. Is this humility? Peaceful resting in God's mercy? Perhaps. More likely spiritual sleepiness. More likely a failure to recognize and follow my own best interests.

I point out the newly noticed steps to Nate. He is delighted and bounds toward them. We climb up, pass through a short tunnel, and then step onto the place that everyone—except the ignorant and too easily satisfied—comes to Skellig Michael to see.

Here, clinging like an ecclesiastical barnacle to the sheer cliffs, is the tiny monastic village. It comprises six stone huts, two oratories, two cisterns, the foundation of a later medieval church, and a graveyard with eroded stone slabs and crosses. The huts have rectangular bases and beehive-shaped roofs, their flat stones held together only by that accommodation to gravity known as corbelling. Four of them have maintained the structural integrity imparted to them at the time of their making. They still stand fourteen centuries later, without mortar or prop, because they were built realistically. That is, they were built in keeping with the vectors of force inherent in the pull of the earth on everything that aspires to rise above it. They work with, not in defiance of, what is. May your life and mine be so constructed.

On the exterior of the monks' cells, stone pegs protrude here and there. Perhaps they held sod or thatch in place, a small allowance for the harsh winter winds in a place where there were never any fires or hot food or any sources of heat beyond the sun and their own bodies. The lack of warming fire is hard enough to imagine in spring and fall, but think of a harsh, North Atlantic winter. Some speculate that the monks may have left the island in winter, but that is more a testimony to what we would do than a reflection of any historical data.

The placement of the monastic site on the southeast side of the north peak, however, may itself have been a minimal concession to comfort. The winds strike the base of the island six hundred feet below and ride the stone straight up into the sky. Set back slightly from the cliff face, the cells and oratories enjoy a microclimate that is slightly milder than the rest of the island. It heartens me that perhaps they did not think it a sin to ease the conditions just a bit.

They did not build the monastery here because this site provided a piece of flatness on the island. Only extensive retaining walls, constructed one must imagine with their hearts in their throats, make possible the buildings at this place. Just beyond the outside retaining wall is a long drop into the sea that would give you just enough time to briefly review your relationship with God and man before you entered eternity.

Nate and I look into each cell and then into the larger oratory shaped like an upturned boat. It is dark and does not feel holy. I try to picture the monks here at worship. Their daily offices, the six appointed times of formal worship (a seventh added in the seventh century) centered on recitations from the Psalms, sometimes as many as seventy-five of them in one service. Novices newly entered into the monastic life, usually between the ages of fifteen and seventeen, would have first memorized all of the poems of the Psalter. A mighty feat by our standards—my students think themselves tortured when required to memorize seventy-five words of poetry—but not difficult for an oral culture that preserved all that it knew in the mind and passed it on with the tongue.

In addition to chanting psalms together, the monks would have readings from the Old and New Testament, pray, and sometimes sing hymns. Their prayers were for themselves and the world and the world's leaders. At various times they would perform their worship on their knees with arms outstretched in the crossvigil position, imitating the crucified Christ. Other times they would prostrate themselves completely on the floor.

Nothing about standing in their oratory inclines me to prostrate myself, or even say a prayer. I am not a good pilgrim. The hoped-for feelings never come on cue. They did not when once I visited Dachau, another terrible-holy place, and they do not now.

But then I see the little window in the eastern wall. I walk over to it and look out. There in the cemetery just behind the oratory is an ancient cross, apparently marking the grave of one of those early monks. And behind the cross is the sky and sea, and in the sea, like a waiting companion, is a smaller companion island, Little Skellig.

It strikes me that this view, tiny window framing sea and island (and cross?), has not changed since the day the oratory was enclosed. On that day this space was marked off as a sacred place within a sacred place, a kind of holy of holies. The monks are long-since departed, but perhaps they left behind more than stones.

ℵ

As Nate and I sit among the beehive huts, looking over the graves of ancient monks to Little Skellig in the sea beyond, we are joined by fellow pilgrims. Some blond-haired Germans or Scandinavians emerge from the tunnel, perhaps distant relatives of earlier Viking visitors. We nod at each other, separated by language but not, it may be, by quest.

We decide to leave the monastery site to them. Skellig Michael is not a place that improves with company, beyond a friend or two. It's time anyway to return to our boat. I see it down below as we come again to Christ's Saddle and then begin to descend the southern steps.

Partway down, those steps take a sharp turn to the right, and at that point is a protruding weathered rock that I imagine to be a medieval Station of the Cross. I tell Nate to stand in front of it so I can take a picture. He looks a bit Viking-like himself: tall, wild red hair, and cunning smile. I am glad he has come with me on this pilgrimage to Skellig Michael. And I am glad we are leaving.

BROTHER JOHN
(From Powerofpurpose.org)

August Turak

In any case, I feel I can personally guarantee that St. Thomas Aquinas loved God, because for the life of me I cannot help loving St. Thomas.
—FLANNERY O'CONNER

Uncertainty as to life's purpose is much in vogue today. So too are the relativistic notions that would consign life's purpose to a matter of taste. The agony of life is uncertainty and the rationalization is that uncertainty is certain. However, the plain truth is that for all our anguish we treasure uncertainty. Doubt forestalls action. The problem with life's purpose is that we know damn well what it is but are unwilling to face the changes in our lives that a commitment to self-transcendence, to being the best human being we could possibly be, would entail. It wearies us just thinking about it. So we rationalize that it's all "relative," or that we're already doing enough and don't have time. Worst of all we rationalize that those who do accept the challenges inherent in self-transcendence are uniquely gifted and specially graced.

It was eight in the evening on Christmas Eve, and I was waiting for Mass to begin. This was my third Christmas retreat at Mepkin Abbey monastery and my third Christmas Eve Mass. Mepkin Abbey sits on 3,132 acres shaded by towering mossy oaks running along the Cooper River just outside Charleston, South Carolina. Once the estate of

Henry and Clare Boothe Luce, it is now a sanctuary for thirty or so Trappist monks living a life of contemplative prayer according to the arduous Rule of St. Benedict.

Already eighteen days into my retreat, I was finally getting used to getting up at three in the morning for Vigils. However I also knew that by the time this special Mass ended at ten-thirty it would be well after our usual bedtime of eight o'clock. The church was hushed and dark, and two brothers began lighting the notched candles lining the walls as Gregorian chant sung by the hidden choir wafted in from the chapel. This chapel, a favorite meditation spot for the monks, sits just off the main sanctuary.

The magic of these pre-Mass rituals quickly had me feeling like I was floating just above my seat. Soon I was drifting back to my first service ever at Mepkin, when Brother Robert, catching me completely off guard, urgently whispered from his adjacent stall, "The chapel is open all night!" This man, a chapel denizen who sleeps barely three hours a night, was apparently so convinced that this was the answer to my most fervent prayer that all I could do was nod knowingly as if to say "Thank God!"

The sound of the rain pelting down on the copper roof of the church on this cold December evening drew me from my reveries, and I noticed with the trace of a smile that I was nervous. I had calmly lectured to large audiences many times, yet I was, as usual, worried that I would somehow screw up the reading that Brother Stan had assigned me for Mass. But reading at Mepkin, especially at Christmas, is such an honor.

I felt that my reading came off very well. Returning to my seat I guess I was still excited because, heedless of the breach of etiquette that speaking at Mass implied, I leaned over and asked Brother Boniface for his opinion. Brother Boniface is Mepkin's ninety-one-year-old statesman, barber, baker, and stand-up comic. He manages these responsibilities despite a painful arthritis of the spine that has left him doubled over and reduced his walk to an inching shuffle. Swiveling his head on his short bent body in order to make eye contact, Boniface lightly touched my arm with his gnarled fingers and gently whispered through his German accent, "You could've been a little slower . . . and a little louder."

After Mass I noticed that the rain had stopped. I headed for the little Christmas party for monks and guests in the dining hall or refectory. Mepkin is a Trappist or Cistercian monastery, and its official name, "The Order of the Cistercians of the Strict Observance (OCSO)," is taken seriously. Casual talking is actively discouraged and even the vegetarian meals are eaten in strict silence. Parties are decidedly rare and not to be missed.

It was a fine affair consisting of light conversation, mutual Christmas wishes, and various Boniface-baked cookies and cakes along with apple cider. Mostly I just basked in the glow of congeniality that I had come to associate so well with Mepkin.

I didn't stay long. It was almost midnight, and after a long day of eight church services, packing eggs, mopping floors, feeding logs into the woodburning furnace, and helping Father Guerric put up Christmas trees, I was asleep on my feet.

I said my good-byes and headed for my room several hundred yards away. Halfway to the refectory door I heard the resurgent rain banging on the roof reminding me that I had forgotten to bring an umbrella. Opening the door I was cursing and resigning myself to a miserable hike and a wet monastic guest habit for morning services, when something startled me and left me squinting into the night. As my eyes adjusted, I made out a dim figure standing under an umbrella outlined by the rain and glowing in the light from the still-open door. It was Brother John in a thin monastic habit, his slouched sixty-year-old body ignoring the cold.

"Brother John! What are you doing?"

"I'm here to walk the people who forgot their umbrellas back to their rooms," he replied softly.

Flicking on his flashlight we wordlessly started off sharing that single umbrella. For my part I was so stunned by this timely offer that I couldn't speak. For in a monastery whose Cistercian motto is "prayer and work" and where there are no slackers, no one works harder than Brother John. He rises before three in the morning to make sure coffee is there for everyone, and is still working after most of his brethren have retired.

Brother John is also what might be termed Mepkin's foreman. After morning Mass the monks without regular positions line up in a room off the church for work assignments, and with several thousand acres full of buildings, machinery, and a farm with forty-thousand chickens there is plenty to do. (As a daily fixture at the grading house packing and stacking eggs thirty dozen to a box, I could easily skip this ritual. I never do. Perhaps it is the way Brother John lights up when I reach the front of the line, touches me ever so lightly on the shoulder, and whispers "grading house" that brings me back every morning. Perhaps it is the humility I feel when he thanks me as if I were doing him a personal favor. . . .) Yet Brother John keeps it all in his head. Every light bulb that flickers out somewhere is his responsibility. He supervises when possible and delegates where he can, but as he is always short-handed, he is constantly jumping in himself at some critical spot. Throughout the monastery the phones ring incessantly with someone on the line asking, "Is John there?" or "Have you seen John?" And through it all, his Irish good humor and gentleness never fades or even frays.

Now after just such a day, four hours after his usual bedtime, and forty years into his monastic hitch, here was Brother John eschewing Boniface's baking, a glass of cider, and a Christmas break in order to walk me back to my room under a shared umbrella.

When we reached the church I reassured him several times that I could cut through to my room on the other side before he relented. But as I opened the door of the church something made me turn, and I continued to watch his flashlight as he hurried back for another pilgrim until its glow faded into the night. When I reached my room, I guess I wasn't as sleepy as I thought. I sat on the edge of my bed in the dark for what I can say with some conviction was a very long time.

꙳

Over the next week I went about my daily routine at Mepkin as usual, but inside I was deeply troubled. I was obsessed with Brother John. On one hand he represented everything I had ever longed for, and on the other all that I had ever feared. I'd read Christian mystics say that God is both terrible and fascinating, and for me Brother John became both.

Of course, this had nothing to do with the fact that he was a monk and I was not. On the contrary, Brother John was fascinating precisely because I intuited that to live as he did, to have his quiet peace and effortless love, had nothing to do with being a monk and was available to us all.

But Brother John was also terrible because he was a living breathing witness to my own inadequacies. Like Alkibiades in Plato's *Symposium,* speaking of the effect Socrates had on him, I had only to picture Brother John under his umbrella to feel as if "life is not worth living the way I live it." I was terrified that if I ever did decide to follow the example of Brother John, I would either fail completely or at best be faced with a life of unremitting effort without Brother John's obvious compensations. I imagined dedicating my life to others, to self-transcendence, without ever finding that inner spark of eternity that so obviously made Brother John's life the easiest and most natural life I had ever known. Perhaps his peace and effortless love were not available to *all* but only to *some*. Perhaps I just didn't have what it takes.

Finally, I asked Father Christian if he could spare a few minutes. Father Christian is Mepkin's feisty, eighty-eight-year-old former abbot, and my irreplaceable spiritual director. Slight and lean, his head is shaven and he wears a bushy chest-length beard which he never cuts. When I commented that his beard didn't seem to be getting any longer, he regretfully said that his beard had stopped growing and added, "While in the popular mind the final length of my beard depends on my longevity, in actuality it depends on my genetics." Fluent in French and Latin and passable in Greek, he acquired Ph.D.s in philosophy, theology, and canon law as a Franciscan before entering Mepkin. His learning, his direct yet gentle manner, and his obvious personal spirituality make him an exceptional spiritual director. And while he grouses once in a while about the bottomless demand for this direction, I've never known him to turn anyone away.

I told Father Christian of my experience with Brother John, and I told him that it had left me in an unsettled state. I wanted to elaborate, but he interrupted me. "So you noticed did you? Amazing how many people take something like that for granted in life. John's a saint, you know."

Then seeming to ignore my predicament he launched into a story about a Presbyterian minister having a crisis of faith and leaving the ministry. The man was a friend of his, and Christian took his crisis so seriously that he actually left the monastery and traveled to his house in order to do what he could. The two men spent countless hours in fruitless theological debate. Finally dropping his voice Christian looked the man steadily in the face and said, "Bob, is everything in your life all right?" The minister said everything was fine. But the minister's wife called Christian a few days later. She had overheard Christian's question and her husband's answer, and she told Father Christian that the minister was having an affair and was leaving her as well as his ministry.

Christian fairly spat with disgust, "I was wasting my time. Bob's problem was that he couldn't take the contradiction between his preaching and his living. So God gets the boot. Remember this, all philosophical problems are at heart moral problems. It all comes down to how you intend to live your life."

We sat silently for a few minutes while Christian cooled off. Maybe he finally took pity on the guy or maybe it was something he saw in my face, but when he spoke the anger in his clear blue eyes had been replaced by a gentle compassion. "You know, you can call it Original Sin, you can call it any darn thing you want to for that matter, but deep down inside every one of us knows something's twisted. Acknowledging that fact, refusing to run away from it, and deciding to deal with it is the beginning of the only authentic life there is. All evil begins with a lie. The biggest evil comes from the biggest lies, and the biggest lies are the ones we tell ourselves. And we lie to ourselves because we're afraid to take ourselves on."

Getting up from his chair, he went to a file cabinet in the corner of his office and took out a folded piece of paper.

Turning, he handed it to me and said, "I know how you feel. You're wondering if you have what it takes. Well, God and you both have some work to do, but I'll say this for you, you're doing your best to look things square in the face."

As he walked out the door I opened the paper he had given me. There, neatly typed by his ancient manual typewriter on plain white paper, was my name in all caps followed by these words from Pascal.

"You would not seek Me if you had not already found Me, and you would not have found Me if I had not first found you."

※

On close inspection, so much of our indecisiveness concerning life's purpose is little more than a variation on the minister's so-called theological doubts. Ultimately it is fear that holds us back, and we avoid this fear through rationalization. We are afraid that if we ever did commit to emulating the Brother Johns of the world that we would merely end up like the Presbyterian minister: pulled apart between the poles of how we *are* living and how we *ought* to live and unable to look away. We are afraid that if we ever did venture out we would find ourselves with the worst of both worlds. On one hand we would learn too much about life to return to our comfortable illusions, and on the other we would learn too much about ourselves to hope for success.

However, in our fear we forget the miraculous.

This fear of the change we need to make in our lives reminds me of an old friend who, though in his thirties and married for some time, was constantly fighting with his wife over her desire to have a baby. Every time he thought of changing into a father the walls closed in. Fatherhood, he thought, was nothing more than dirty diapers, stacks of bills, sleepless nights, and doting in-laws in every spare bed and couch. Fatherhood meant an end to spontaneous weekends and evenings with the guys. It also meant trading in his sports car for a minivan and a bigger life insurance policy. It was all so overwhelming.

Then one day he gave in. He set his jaw and made the decision to transform himself from a man into a father. He took the chance that he would find himself with all the responsibility of fatherhood and with none of its compensations. Then on another day, his wife handed him his newborn boy.

Unexpectedly an inner alchemy began, and something came over him from a direction he didn't know existed. He melted and magically the baby gave birth to a father. He was so full of love for this child that he didn't know what to do with himself. While he once feared losing sleep he began checking his baby so often that the baby lost sleep. He found himself full of boundless gratitude for his rebirth, regret for the fool he was, and compassion for single friends who simply couldn't understand. He called it a miracle.

Similarly, we must take a chance and act on faith. We must give in, make the commitment, and be willing to pay the price. We must commit to becoming one with that passive spark of divinity longing for actuality that Thorton Wilder in *Our Town* describes so well:

> Now there are some things we all know but we don't take'm out and look at'm very often. We all know that *something* is eternal. . . . everybody knows in their bones that *something* is eternal and that something has to do with human beings. All the greatest people ever lived have been telling us that for five thousand years and yet you'd be surprised how people are always losing hold of it. There's something

way down deep that's eternal about every human being.

We must commit to facing our doubts, limitations, and self-contradictions head on while holding on to this voice of eternity. This eternal voice is urging us to take a chance on an unknown outcome in much the same way that nature's voice urged my friend to take a chance on a new life. And we must fight distraction, futility, rationalization, and fatigue at every step.

From this side of the chasm we may react with dismay at all the work involved in never again "losing hold of it." From this side it may be hard to imagine that just as changing a diaper can be magically transformed from drudgery to an effortless privilege so can standing outside in the rain for others. But to experience the magic of this transformation we must put aside these doubts. We must resolve to act decisively while trusting in the aid of something we don't understand and can never predict. We must open ourselves up to the miraculous, to grace.

Working toward this miraculous transformation, rebirth, or inner alchemy is the true purpose of life. This transformation is what the West calls "conversion" and the East "enlightenment," and is the fruit of our commitment to the authentically purposeful life that Father Christian described so well. It is this transformation that turns work into effortless privilege, makes the unnatural values of Brother John second nature, and proves that the answer to the monk's last prayer each night at Compline for a "restful night and a peaceful death" is eternally ours. And when we're ready, Brother John will be waiting for us eager to share this miraculous umbrella. Like him we will be utterly grateful for who we have become, remorseful for who we were, and compassionate toward those who do not understand.

I am not a monk, but I spend enough time at Mepkin Abbey that Father Feliciano introduced me to a visitor recently and followed it with, "He's always here." I am often asked why I go. I go because Brother John loves God so much he doesn't know what to do with himself. He doesn't know what to do with himself so he stands outside on a cold Christmas night with an umbrella waiting. Waiting to offer us some protection and human comfort on our long journey home.

SPOKANE

A Triptych

(From *Image*)

Paul J. Willis

I Should Have Talked

In his book *Desert Solitaire*, Edward Abbey refers offhand-
edly to American evangelicalism as a form of mental illness.
I am hoping he is wrong. And it seems to me that Abbey
himself, in his many barbs directed at his childhood faith,
cannot quite turn his eyes away from it. In this, I think, he is
like Mark Twain—both of them Christ-haunted in twisted
and peculiar ways. If there is a mental illness of faith, there
may also be a mental illness of lost faith.

But Abbey's comment invites agreement, even from
evangelicals. At the very least, evangelicalism seems to
encourage strange forms of delusional, masochistic behavior. This literally came home to me some years ago, during
the time my wife and I were still in school, when a sadly
afflicted man spent the night with us in Spokane. Sharon and
I picked him up on a grimy winter afternoon at the bus station. He had come from Pullman, eighty miles south. His
wife, Jill, an acquaintance of Sharon's, had asked if Jerry
could stay overnight before flying out to Toronto. I had met
Jerry the month before, just before we had moved north to
Spokane. He had been witnessing door-to-door with book-
lets from the Seventh-Day Adventist Church, and had

knocked on our door as well. One look at his weak eyes and childlike face and I knew he was a little off. Sharon told me she didn't know all the details, but Jill had told her that Jerry was now mentally ill and hadn't held a job for the last two years. They lived on unemployment.

Jerry stepped off the bus carrying a bulging suitcase with broken clasps; it was held together with knotted twine. He spoke softly, ending almost every sentence with *you know.* "I appreciate this, you know." We drove to our apartment, where he sat on the couch and said little. "That's what I do most, you know," he said during dinner. "Just sit on the couch. Don't seem to have the energy." While helping me wash the dishes, he confided that he planned to enter the ministry. It was hard to know how to reply.

When we finished the dishes, he said, "I'd like to join you in your family worship later this evening, you know."

"Well," I replied, "we were just planning to study tonight, actually."

"We have family worship every night," he said. "We sing some familiar choruses and the kids say their memory verses, you know. Jamie, he can usually say his, but Jay can usually only recognize his verse. Jay's just two, you know. You and Sharon could just pick out some familiar choruses for later on this evening, you know."

As I think about it now, I realize how little it would have cost us to read some scripture and sing some songs with Jerry that night. I'd like to think that today I would have done so. But on that night, out of pure stubbornness, I suppose, not to mention several poems I had to read for my seminar in the pastoral, I ignored his request. At some level, I felt a kind of creeping revulsion. The idea of family worship felt tainted by his mental illness.

When Jerry saw that Sharon and I were intent on our schoolwork, he left to go witnessing in the neighborhood. I cringed as the door closed behind him. What had we unleashed on our block? Earlier in the evening he had told me about a man on the bus with whom he had shared the gospel. "I offered him the booklet and he took it," he said with a hopeful look.

Over Christmas Jerry had been in the hospital for tests. He had spent several hours lying in a room with a tube all the way down his throat. Next to him had been a man about to go into surgery. A month later Jerry heard fourth-hand about a man who had died at the hospital. Jerry was sure it was the man he had lain next to for those few hours.

"I should have talked to him," he said. "I've learned my lesson now—I should have talked to him."

"How could you have talked to him with a tube down your throat?" I asked.

"I should have talked to him," Jerry said.

When Jerry got back from witnessing, he returned a call from his wife. "I love you, honey," he said, and then laughed a three-beat, quiet, crazy, embarrassed laugh: "Hee-hee-hee." A minute later he said, "I love you, honey. Hee-hee-hee." He said it exactly the same way.

Then Jerry went out to run for exercise. He wore his winter coat, checked slacks, and leather street shoes. He wouldn't borrow my tennis shoes and sweatpants. Soon enough he came back and took a shower and padded around in his pajamas. Just before going to bed, he settled down for a little while and read a book called *The Christian Father*. The next day he would fly to Canada to stay with his parents for a month. I hoped that when I drove him to the airport in the morning we could have some kind of friendly talk. I think I felt ashamed of myself for not warming up to him.

In the morning, however, the streets were thick with fresh snow. Getting Jerry to the airport was suddenly going to be a challenge. As best I could I put on our ancient chains. We drove through fishtailing traffic on the interstate, my arms rigid, and a loose set of links on the left rear tire mercilessly flogged the fender. The whole way there, I didn't say a word.

Just this morning, twenty years later, I happened to have breakfast with a couple who have taken care of five mentally handicapped adults in their home for the last fifteen years. What manner of love is this? I thought. Other friends have done this kind of thing as well—even an English professor friend—and my wife has worked off and on in group homes for the retarded. And of course there is the famous example of Henri Nouwen, the Catholic theologian who devoted the last years of his life to serving the mentally disabled. Perhaps it is true that evangelicalism in its more extreme forms offers a ready means of expression for the unhinged among us. But perhaps it is more true that the mentally ill offer to us the plainest picture of ourselves, our deepest longing for a love we hope both to know and to share. If so, I hope I get another try.

And You Visited Me

When I showed up for my two o'clock tutorial with Dr. Jordan, I found he was gone. A note on the door said he was ill. So I went across the street to the university library to ask his wife, a librarian, how he was doing. Not well, she said, and gave me the name of a hospital near Spokane, eighty or ninety miles away. I knew he was not a healthy man, but she wasn't very clear about the details of his illness. Would he like a visitor? Since I lived in Spokane, it would not be difficult for me to see him. His wife said a visit might be just the thing. But she didn't look me in the eye.

So three days later, after I had returned home from my weekly stint of tutorials and seminars, I drove out to the named hospital. It rested on the north shore of a quiet lake among ponderosas, spreading lawns, and mossy granite out-croppings. I parked the car and walked past a brown-brick wing behind a row of cedar trees. At the visitor registration desk I gave my name and asked to see Rath Jordan.

The receptionist looked through her papers and said, "I'm sorry, but there is no Rath Jordan here."

I asked her to check again.

"No, sorry. No one by that name."

"There must be some mistake," I said.

"No mistake," she said less pleasantly.

But I didn't leave, and eventually she left her desk and disappeared into another room behind her.

When I had proposed a tutorial in the short story in January, Dr. Jordan had responded to me with a similarly abrupt *no*. He was too busy trying to complete a freshman introduction to literature text for Random House, which, he informed me, two other professors in the department had dropped in his lap because they were too damn lazy to keep up their end of the work. "In two years, neither of them ever wrote a single word." He said *a single word* with slowed, staccato emphasis.

Furthermore, he was too ill to do a study with me. His pancreas and adrenal glands did not function properly, and as a result his body chemistry was precarious. Periodically he would lose all "higher cognitive function." As it was, his mind did not work properly until noon. So there would be no tutorial. That was clear.

Could he recommend other professors, key readings? He went down the list of names carefully: "Too limited in his reading; no real penetration of thought; more of a writer than a critic." No, he couldn't fully recommend anyone. Then he pulled out one book, another, and another, warmed to his most favorite of subjects, waxed eloquent, gained in his face a glow of passion. I excused myself to turn in a paper and then returned. He looked up like a boy who has just decided to play hooky.

"Let's do it," he said.

And so we met for an hour and a half, every Tuesday afternoon. By March we had read Chekhov, Crane, Verga, Fitzgerald. Chekhov was his love.

"'The Lady with the Pet Dog,'" he liked to say, "was Chekhov's way of telling Tolstoy how life really worked. You can't impose a smug moral order the way Tolstoy does in *Anna Karenina.*"

"Yes," I liked to reply, "but what if Chekhov has subtracted something that Tolstoy did not impose, but merely recognized as inherent?"

After a long wait, the receptionist returned from the back room with surprising evidence of the existence of Rath Jordan. She gave me directions to his ward, where I met him in an old, dirty hallway. He was fully clothed, thin, and pale, and shook my hand warmly. Odd-looking people sauntered about, also dressed in street clothes. They wore strange gazes and expressions. It very belatedly dawned on me what kind of hospital this was. Dr. Jordan ushered me into a dusty lounge, and we sat down on some grimy rubber furniture in playschool blues and greens and yellows. An AM radio blared, and several men played billiards on a battered table.

"Sorry I missed my appointment on Tuesday," he said, "but my body chemistry went completely topsy-turvy. When that happens, I become unavoidably suicidal."

I started inside, but tried not to show it.

"I've just been released from seventy-two hours of intensive observation—along with some pretty hardcore people. I talked to a guy this morning who wired a shotgun under a store manager's throat. He connected the trigger to his own hand with an electrical cord. When the police gunned him down, he automatically set off the shotgun."

I wondered why he was telling me this. Was it to show that he himself was not so deranged as that—or to show that we all were?

"We line up for medication here," he said. "Just like in the *Cuckoo's Nest*. I feel like I'm in that movie sometimes."

I had brought a volume of Fitzgerald, just in case he wanted to talk literature. He did—very badly. We arranged for a small, dingy coffee room to ourselves. It had one, tall, narrow window of many small panes; I wondered if the latticework was an iron grill. We managed a discussion about one Fitzgerald story, "The Diamond as Big as the Ritz," and then he wandered onto the turf of other writers. Clearly, he enjoyed talking. Every once in a while I would interject an observation apropos of the subject he had happened upon. He would stop and say, "Yes, I hadn't thought of that. Very good!" I suppose that this return to the role of caretaker felt reassuring to him. The spell was broken only once, by an attendant with a paper cup of water and a pair of pills. He took them obediently.

Soon afterward our time ended. He put his hand to his head and said, "You'd better leave. I'm getting tired. I can handle being intellectually tired—that's one thing. Or being physically tired—that's almost pleasant. It's being emotionally wiped out that gets me."

He asked if I could come back every other day—he'd have to be here two weeks. "We'd get a lot done that way," he said. Then he apologized for not having reviewed the stories. He wasn't allowed any books.

"I'll let you borrow this one," I offered.

"Okay," he said. "I think I can keep it locked up safe."

Before I left he took me by the arm and said how good it was that I had come. He held my gaze, and his eyes were weak and watery. "If anyone asks about me," he said less certainly, "tell them I'm getting much better and hope to be back soon."

Amo, Amas, Amat

In those student years that we lived in Spokane, Sharon and I eventually moved to a blonde-brick apartment house just west of downtown. Just across the hall from us lived an elderly couple from Plentywood, Montana. Henry Raaen was a Norwegian bachelor farmer until the age of forty-nine, when he married Minnie, a schoolteacher. She had played the organ at the Lutheran church where he had sung in the choir. They celebrated their fiftieth anniversary the summer after we met them. Then Mr. Raaen turned one hundred, and Mrs. Raaen a spry eighty-seven.

One evening they invited us over for dessert, and by request I brought along my textbook for the Latin I was starting to learn. Mrs. Raaen had been a passionate teacher of Latin, and she often complained, or gloated rather, that young people these days were no longer interested in the Latin tongue. When I handed her my text, she found a line in the preface that she read to us with sad glee: "It is notorious that every year increasing numbers of students enter college without Latin."

She turned the pages slowly, looking up to tell us about a former teacher of her acquaintance who could not speak of the death of Julius Caesar without breaking into tears. "Sometimes," said Mrs. Raaen, "I lay awake at night reviewing my conjugations."

Then she got to the first set of verbs in the book. "Oh, yes," she said approvingly. Then, "Henry, do you remember the first conjugation?"

Up to this point, Henry had held a rigid silence. Part blind, part deaf, chock-full of arthritis, he sat erect in a red sweater and tie. Even the tops of his ears held deep, pale wrinkles. I wondered how his hundred-year-old mind worked.

He answered his wife like a cannon shot: "*Amo-amas-amat-amamus-amatis-amant!*"

Mrs. Raaen paged through the text for another five minutes, fondly absorbed. "Yes," she said, "I recognize most of the words on every page. But it would be too hard to get it all back. Too hard now to get it all back." Her face and voice were sadly resigned.

"May I make a motion," croaked Mr. Raaen, "that we put the Latin aside and proceed with dessert?"

Mrs. Raaen agreed, but then she happened upon the vocabulary index in the back, and the keyed exercises that go with every lesson. Dessert did not come for some time.

A few weeks later we invited the Raaens to our apartment to listen to *A Prairie Home Companion* on the radio. We thought they would be the perfect audience. For two hours they sat with us politely in our living room, the volume turned up very high, while Garrison Keillor said droll things about Lutherans and Norwegian bachelor farmers. Mr. and Mrs. Raaen gave the program their complete and stolid attention. They never laughed. They never smiled. When Garrison Keillor at last said, "Good night, everybody. Good night, now," Henry and Minnie rose to their feet with a kind of puzzled dignity and thanked us for having them. Then they left. *Exeunt ambo.*

We later moved just upstairs from them, and from time to time we would hear a crash from below, indicating that Mr. Raaen had fallen off the toilet or out of bed. I would hurry downstairs and restore Mr. Raaen to something like tranquility, and life would go on. Occasionally an ambulance would come to the door, an occasion that Mrs. Raaen always met with sureness and solemnity. She would follow the stretcher out the door with head held high, arm in arm with the paramedic. This was it, she was thinking. After all these years, the final act, and she would march out like royalty. The fact that she got to repeat this performance several times in no way lessened the effect. She only improved with practice.

A few weeks before Mr. Raaen turned 103, just before Christmas, Sharon gave birth to our first child, a baby boy. Soon after we had brought him home, we took Jonathan down to the Raaens's apartment and into their bedroom, where Mr. Raaen lay cadaverously beneath the covers. With some effort he propped himself up and stretched out a hand of blessing upon the head of our little son. I have forgotten to say that Mr. Raaen was a giant man, well over six feet in length, with huge, horny, spreading hands. Could Simeon in the Temple, when he met with the holy infant, have looked or acted any other way?

Then Mr. Raaen held out a five-dollar bill that he had hidden in the blankets. "From the oldest man in the building to the youngest!" he shouted.

That next year, of course, he died.

Nunc dimittis servum tuum Domine,
Secundum verbum tuum in pace.
Lord, now let your servant depart,
According to your word, in peace.

WEDDING INSANITY

(From *The Cresset*)

Lauren F. Winner

In her new memoir, *Bride in Overdrive*, WeddingChannel.com columnist Jorie Green Mark chronicles her "journey into wedding insanity and back." The story opens with Barry's proposal, Jorie's enthusiastic acceptance, and a sparkly diamond. Then the real fun begins: Jorie plunges into the stacks of bridal magazines she's been hoarding for months, and realizes that "*It was finally my turn to be Queen for a Day*"—this revelation comes in a chapter called "It's My Wedding, and I'll Whine if I Want To." Jorie will float into the Ritz-Carlton in Vera Wang silk (or maybe a gown by Amsale, or Richard Tyler; there are just so many options!). She will serve lobster and prime rib. Her engraved Crane's invitations will boast "a silver foil lining on the inner envelope, and an '*M*' monogram seal—an *M* for Mark, *M* for Marriage, *M* for My Marvelous Day."

Of course, Jorie plays the self-involved prima donna only in chapter three, for the memoir turns not only on the details of her marvelous day (a day that took sixteen months to plan) but also on her gradual move from a place of willful self-entitlement to one of compromise and cooperation. First, Jorie, following the wise counsel of anonymous online interlocutors, realizes that she can't have both the lobster and the foil liners, because they exceed the limits of the budget her eminently reasonable and generous father has set for her. Next, though initially devastated when Barry vetoes the font she has painstakingly selected for the wedding invitations, Jorie proves able to simmer down and find a font they both love. Gradually, she even stops calling the event "my wedding" and begins calling it "ours."

I have spent this summer, like almost every other summer, attending a hectic round of weddings, sometimes more than one squeezed into a single weekend. At wedding after wedding, as I stood in my high heels munching miniature quiches and juggling my drink and my hors d'oeuvres and making small talk with people I'd never see again, I thought about my own wedding, a feast my husband and I celebrated a little less than a year ago. I compared our delicious country apple wedding cake to the chocolate/apricot/raspberry mousse confections my friends had chosen to serve at their nuptial galas. I pondered our wedding presents with an eye toward regifting (a verb I didn't learn until I became A Bride). And it occurred to me that I should organize our expensive and artful wedding photographs in the trendy scrapbook I purchased last September, but still haven't quite seemed to carve out the time to do. This event which consumed so many hours in preparation already feels a little far away for renewed devotion.

There was, of course, much that was astonishing about our wedding. Griff and I served as chalice bearers during the celebration of Holy Communion that concluded the marriage service. Yes, I was terrified I was going to spill the blood of Christ on my white, cotton organdy gown; but, dry-cleaning nightmares notwithstanding, the serving of communion wine was, for me, the best part of the day. In serving communion, I suddenly stopped being a plastic figure atop a wedding cake, a comely but passive doll to whom something remarkable was being done. For a few moments, Griff and I were transformed into experts of ritual who could give back to our community some of what had just been given to us. It was, as one of my five-year-old Sunday schoolers said, really cool.

✤

Our wedding reception, on the other hand—and the reception is generally what people mean when they talk of "weddings"—seems like something of a non sequitur. For starters, the reception did not go off without a hitch. (Take as synecdoche the fact that there weren't nearly enough chairs and that the caterers ran out of champagne flutes long before the evening ended.) But more important, here in the midst of a first year of marriage, I look around my complicated, hard, and wonderful married life, and I wonder about the logic of my lovely wedding reception. What do the lace and the celadon green boutonnières, the damask tablecloths and finger food, and all those champagne bubbles have to do with marriage?

There is an answer to that question, of course. Marriages are great things, and they should be celebrated. But it seems that the celebrations that do the best work are those whose accoutrements bear a real and deep connection to the thing they are ritualizing and celebrating.

And so my concern about contemporary weddings is not primarily the predictable anxieties about the cost (though I've not yet made my peace with the fact that instead of having a wedding reception, my family could have sent a deserving teenager to an in-state college for four years). It is rather the disjuncture between weddings and the marriages they make. For contemporary weddings are all about fantasy; the fifty-billion-dollar-a-year wedding industry tells women that, in Jorie Mark's phrase, "it [is] glamorous to be in love, to look out at your surroundings through a filmy layer of tulle."

✳

We could describe marriage with such adjectives as "wonderful," "life-giving," and, at times, "fun." But *glamorous?* I think not. To carry on Jorie's textile metaphor, marriages are less about tulle than—oh, cotton, and wool, and the occasional bit of raw silk, and sometimes some velvet. Marriage is not a continuation of the heady bliss of engagement (and, in fact, engagement brings its own unique stresses and strains); rather, it is about community and domesticity. In the resounding phrase of the *Book of Common Prayer,* we enter into marriage for "mutual joy; for the help and comfort given one another in prosperity and adversity; and, when it is God's will, for the procreation of children and their nurture in the knowledge and love of the Lord." The outings, meals, conversations, and sex that weddings inaugurate are not the stuff of whimsy, but of routine (and that "routine" and "domesticity" have become buzz-kills is itself part of the problem).

When Jorie whined, she was merely following the beguiling instructions of all those bridal magazines, ritual primers that tell us to be, within the confines of our budget, queen for a day. (Or perhaps "princess" is better, for as Caitlin Flanagan observed in 2001, our current bloated wedding daydreams may date to 1981, when American girls all over the country set their alarms and rose in the middle of the night in order to "witness Charles and Diana plighting their troth in real time.") Princess or queen, this is an odd mind-set with which to enter a marriage, the arena where bending one's will is not only required, it is in fact part of the point. Marriage—Christian marriage, at any rate—is not merely about "compromise," it is about death to self. We marry not only so that we can have licit sex and raise children, but also because we believe marriage to be one of the institutions God has given us to facilitate our dying to our old selves and prepare us for our eventual resurrection.

If America's culture of conspicuous consumption has exacerbated the dissonance between weddings and marriage, that dissonance is not unique to our era. Apparently brides and grooms in fourth-century Antioch were tempted to throw extravagant wedding feasts, and St. John Chrysostom was prompted to remind them from the pulpit that their weddings would be—or should be—a window into their marriages. When one is preparing a wedding, one ought not "run to your neighbors' houses borrowing extra mirrors, or spend endless hours worrying about dresses." For marriage, insisted Chrysostom, "is a bond, a bond ordained by God. Why then do you celebrate weddings in a silly or immodest manner? Have you no idea what you are doing? You are marrying . . . for the procreation of children and for moderation of life; what is the meaning of these drunken parties with their lewd and disgraceful behavior? You can enjoy a banquet with your friends to celebrate your marriage; I do not forbid this, but why must you introduce all these excesses? . . . Is marriage a comedy? It is a mystery, an image of something far greater. . . . Pagan mysteries are the only ones that involve dancing. We celebrate our mysteries quietly and decently, with reverence and modesty."

Perhaps the most insightful section of Jorie Green Mark's memoir is the last page. Around the time of their first wedding anniversary, Jorie found out she was pregnant. "[A]s we'd soon learn, my efforts to plan a perfect, and I mean *perfect,* wedding—only to learn that this is not an impossible but an undesirable accomplishment—was great preparation for parenthood. Because from the moment my water broke . . . there was very little we could plan. There was very little we could anticipate."

She reads her wedding as a positive preparation for parenthood; through the ups and downs and foibles and disappointments of wedding planning, she learns that she can't orchestrate everything.

But, one might ask, why not re-conceive our weddings with Jorie's first-anniversary epiphany in mind? For Jorie's epiphany tells us much better than *Bride* magazine what marriages are made of.

PICTURING THE PASSION

(From *Image*)

Gregory Wolfe

Now that Mel Gibson's *The Passion of the Christ* has reached thousands of screens around the world and the frenzy of editorializing, pre- and post-release, has died down, two of the early questions about the film have been answered. Once the film entered the public domain, most of the fears about whether it was anti-Semitic dissipated, leaving only some concern about the possibility that in certain parts of the globe anti-Semites might use the film to incite violence. The other question—would *The Passion*'s graphic violence keep people away from the theaters—has been answered with a resounding no. The numbers are such that any attempt to characterize interest in the film as mere curiosity strikes me as strained. Indeed, the controversy over Gibson's film has become something of a mirror-image of the earlier culture-war shouting match over Martin Scorsese's *The Last Temptation of Christ:* in the case of the present film, it is the critics who have turned up their noses and the public who have filled the theaters.

I was prepared to dislike this film. Having had a few unpleasant run-ins over the years with hyper-traditionalist Catholicism at its most ideological and eccentric, and hearing that Gibson might have a similar worldview, I was ready to seize upon any sign of anti-Semitism, esoteric religious symbolism, or political paranoia. What I encountered was something far more centric, more deeply grounded in the aesthetic and theological traditions of Christianity than I had expected. Disturbing and emotionally draining as *The Passion* may be, it is a remarkable achievement, a daring recovery of iconographic and theological language that had all but disappeared from the public realm.

That the film has its share of flaws and misjudgments I will readily grant. For example, there is the fundamental difficulty of translating the words of the Bible into a different medium. The history of film is strewn with abject failures in this genre, large and small. A few years ago the writer Virginia Stem Owens touched on this issue in a book review of Frederick Buechner's novel, *The Son of Laughter,* which recounts some of the Genesis narrative from Isaac's point of view. In the review, Owens quotes from Erich Auerbach's classic work, *Mimesis,* to make her point:

> *The Son of Laughter* definitely succeeds in terms of entertainment and passionate narrative. Yet, like other novels borrowing from biblical stories, it simply fills in too much, closing the gaps which, Auerbach says, are intended "to overcome our reality." Any reality we add will always be exasperatingly partial. Instead of explaining the biblical world in our terms, we must "fit our own life into its world" and allow ourselves "to be elements in its structure of universal history." The gaps are meant to swallow us.

A director of consummate artistry like Wim Wenders would probably endorse the point Owens made. For someone like Wenders, the frontal approach is doomed to failure: better to refract the ancient story in oblique ways through contemporary narratives that give us situations and characters to which we can relate. The invisible reality of faith is something best made visible when it haunts the edges of consciousness and memory.

However compelling these points may be, it would be obtuse not to recognize that there is a fundamental human need to reimagine the ancient stories in whatever media are available. In the smorgasbord of aesthetic choices, there will always be a corner of the table for more direct approaches, however fraught with risk they may be.

Gibson's use of sustained, graphic violence in *The Passion* is another gamble that many people have questioned. Even a sympathetic Christian viewer like theologian Gil Bailie feels that Gibson miscalculated here. The danger of this level of violence is that it will turn Jesus into the gold medalist in the Olympics of Suffering. Bailie writes:

> Christ's death changed the human condition forever, not because he suffered more than anyone else ever did, but because, as "the Lamb slain from the foundation of the world," he suffered the fate of every victim everywhere. . . . The shocking thing about the cross of Christ is that God's Anointed One dies on it, revealing once and for all the otherwise unimaginable truth about the depths of God's love.

It is at this juncture where one bumps up against the limits of even the best acting and cinematography. Gibson does make an effort to have Jesus look at those around him with ever deepening love and compassion as the Passion progresses. But his film is far more effective in tracing the transformative effect of Christ's sacrifice on bystanders like Simon of Cyrene and the centurion, and on the two Marys, than he is able to convey divinity through his protagonist.

Ultimately, the strongest defense for the use of violence in this film is the issue of sacramentality, the Christian belief that the Incarnation hallows our human, corporeal condition. In the history of the church, Christ is always being etherealized, rendered comfortably abstract, by liberals and conservatives. One of the enduring strengths of *The Passion* is its use of gesture, touch, and gaze to convey presence. Once again, it is the figure of Mary, superbly played by Maia Morgenstern, who conveys this most vividly. When, near the end of the film, Mary kisses her son's foot on the cross, her face is smeared with blood, as if she is drunk on wine—an allusion both to the wedding at Cana and the Eucharist.

Moments like this abound in the film, though they can be hard to retain in the midst of the engulfing horror. But they are there, from the hand of the fallen Magdalene inching across to the foot of her savior (both paralleling and opposing the snake that crawls toward him in Gethsemane) to Mary's homing movements as she hunkers on the ground above the place where her son is being held in the hellish womb of captivity below. When he is given his cross to bear, Jesus hugs it to himself like a man being reunited with his lover. Mary's willing embrace of Christ's suffering—the "Yes" that parallels the Annunciation—gives the film emotional and spiritual ballast.

Gibson's decision to introduce a number of supernatural elements into the story, including the figure of Satan (who does not appear in the Gospel accounts of the Passion), seems to be a crime against the very sacramentalism that otherwise gives the film its power. I wish he had kept the story relentlessly on the human plane, so that by focusing on the visible and tangible, the invisible would register there and there only.

The religion scholar Stephen Prothero has criticized what he calls Gibson's "blood and guts sacramentality." But what other kind is there? If God cannot become present in blood, guts, shit, piss, semen, saliva—He vanishes into the ether. In short, this is not the Messiah of the Jesus Seminar, who increasingly seems to resemble a divinity being graded on a curve. In his *New York Times* op-ed on the film, Kenneth Woodward aptly quoted the famous formula coined by theologian H. Richard Niebuhr to criticize the modern therapeutic vision of Christianity: "A God without wrath brought men without sin into a kingdom without judgment through the ministrations of a Christ without a cross."

Does *The Passion* represent an excessive reaction? Does it signal the resurgence of some sort of dark, atavistic religion? The return of a manly Christ as opposed to a more sensitive and inclusive savior? I'm not so sure. Gibson's Jesus puts me in mind of a column from a British newspaper that my wife once read out loud to me. In an article on the relationship between the sexes in the early 1980s, numerous women were quoted as losing patience with men who had become too accommodating and passive. "I want a man I can push up against," one woman wrote. It seems fair to say that a lot of people today are longing for a Jesus they can push up against.

That unnerves some people, including a number of our cultural gatekeepers. That *The Passion* has violated something akin to a tacit social contract established during the Enlightenment can be seen in a reflective essay by *New York Times* film critic A. O. Scott. He not only argues that the film ignores "pluralism and interreligious politesse" but also says that it dangerously blurs the lines between "sacred and secular." It seems that some of the film's most fervent admirers regard the film not as a work of art but something like the Authorized Version, a videotape of biblical history. Scott also notes, with evident distaste, that some of those involved in making the film had a number of intense spiritual experiences during the production process.

If Scott's argument were merely that some people are naïve and partisan enough to forget that *The Passion* is a work of art, a human artifact, then one could hardly object (although his condescension remains revolting). But Scott goes further, I think, suggesting that it is a sinister development for our society when religious believers develop a devotional attitude toward a work of art. Here I think he is forgetting his history. Until the modern era, very few works of art in the history of man that dealt with religious texts and symbols could be cleanly divided into sacred and secular, aesthetic and liturgical. *The Divine Comedy* is a secular poem, but the hymn to the Virgin in the *Paradiso* can and has been said as a prayer. The same dynamic relationship between the aesthetic and liturgical can be said of many of the classic paintings that Gibson drew on for *The Passion,* from Caravaggio's *Deposition* to the heart-wrenchingly beautiful *Avignon Pietà,* the penultimate image of *The Passion.* In the modern era the same positive tension can be found in paintings by Georges Rouault or poems by Eliot, Auden, or Levertov.

Admittedly, the borderland between art and liturgy is rarely an inspiring place: it's more likely to be populated by kitsch than by works of tragic grandeur. But *The Passion* inhabits that sphere with some distinction; it *is* devotional in nature, an extended cinematic version of the Stations of the Cross.

A. O. Scott feels that *The Passion* changes the cultural rules in a way he finds threatening. In that sense, the film is what the postmodernists might call "transgressive." Of course, that's high praise when intellectuals use the word to denote works that challenge certain traditional values and institutions. But there are times when the word "politesse" is just a euphemism for a particular brand of censorship: in this case, the insistence that the public square be stripped of unsightly expressions of faith.

Roger Ebert called *The Passion* a "personal message film," and there's some truth to that, but not in the sense that one would use that phrase of, say, Oliver Stone. However individual and controversial and subject to criticism his rendition may be, Mel Gibson's message is nourished and shaped by his respect for an ancient tradition. And at the heart of that tradition is the belief in the unimaginable depth of God's passion for us.

IS ART SALVIFIC?

(From *The Hedgehog Review*)

Nicholas Wolterstorff

Late in his career the eminent analytic philosopher of art Monroe Beardsley, a person who avoided overstatement and hyperbole in his writing as if they were mortal sins, published these words:

> The fundamental task of the philosophy of art in our time . . . is to mark out the special sphere of artistic activity, duly recognizing the peculiar and precious character of its contribution to the goodness and significance of life. . . . This theoretical task has as its practical analogue that of finding ways of preserving and enlarging the capacity of the arts to play their distinctive and needed roles in promoting the quality of social life, protecting them against the enormous political and economic forces that constantly threaten to control, distort, repress, or trivialize them.[1]

Four years earlier the Frankfurt School theorist Herbert Marcuse made essentially the same point with words considerably more flamboyant and bearing a much heavier theoretical freight:

The radical qualities of art, that is to say, its indict-
ment of the established reality and its invocation of
the beautiful image of liberation, are grounded precisely in the dimensions where art transcends its
social determination and emancipates itself from the
given universe of discourse and behavior while pre-
serving its overwhelming presence. . . . The inner
logic of the work of art terminates in the emergence
of another reason, another sensibility, which defy the
rationality and sensibility incorporated in the dominant social institutions.[2]

Not many of those presently writing about the arts
would say what Beardsley and Marcuse said twenty-five
years ago. A mood of disappointment has descended; we
live with crushed expectations. That mood of disappointment is nicely caught in the introduction to this issue of *The
Hedgehog Review:*

In the late nineteenth and early twentieth centuries,
there were those who looked to the arts with the
highest expectations, regarding them as a source of
deep personal meaning and public cohesion. From
Romanticism to humanistic Marxism, the hope was
held that the arts would reflect the highest ideals of
humanity in such a way that they would be, in effect,
an alternative expression of transcendence in a secular society.

Yet by the end of the twentieth century, it was
clear that the arts had failed to achieve this promise.

Behind the Romantics' proposal of art as a redemptive
activity, as a replacement for the metanarratives of Christianity and socialism, was an alternative narrative, a *counter-*

narrative. Almost all philosophy of art written over the past two centuries has accepted that counter-narrative, and busied itself with articulating and justifying it. That Grand Modern Narrative of the Arts, as I shall call it, is now sick unto death. Its sickness is the cause of our disappointment. For the narrative was a narrative of salvific hope.

The narrative is not dying because art has not yet saved us. Most religious people are willing to wait a long time for their messiah to arrive. It is dying because, during the quarter of a century that separates our time from the time that Beardsley and Marcuse wrote their words, there has been a sustained assault on the very idea of the artist as the suffering innocent, and on art as transcending our depraved political and economic institutions and practices. Not only do our artists put their wares on the market, like everybody else; but our theorists and critics have rubbed our noses in the racism, sexism, colonialism, and nationalism present in art. Few have been able to keep the faith that this is mere accident. The artist is not someone from heaven; the artist is us. What he makes shows that.

In this essay I want to explore the ways in which, for three centuries now, the Grand Narrative has been intertwined with religious expectations for art. That done, I will propose a better way of thinking of the relation between religion and the arts. The narrative is familiar; for two centuries now it has been an intrinsic component of the mentality of the intelligentsia of the West. Usually it is taken for granted, rather than explicitly noted. For my subsequent purposes it will be important to hold it up for view. I will have to skip all the rich details and the supporting evidence and confine myself to the bare outlines.

The Grand Narrative emerged as an account of the revolutionary development that took place in the arts during the eighteenth century in Western Europe. Any number of writers have described one or another aspect of those developments. In his wonderful essay, "The Modern System of the Arts," Paul Oskar Kristeller traces the slow emergence of our modern concept of the arts;[3] and in two equally wonderful essays, "Art-as-Such: The Sociology of Modern Aesthetics" and "From Addison to Kant: Modern Aesthetics and the Exemplary Art," M. H. Abrams traces some of the crucial shifts that took place in ways of engaging and thinking about what we now call the arts.[4]

I judge the most fundamental development that occurred in the eighteenth century to have been the emergence among the Western European bourgeoisie of perceptual contemplation as their most valued mode of engagement with the arts, and the corresponding emergence into dominance among writers on the arts of what Abrams calls the "contemplation model." Writing about the arts in the West goes all the way back into Greek antiquity; but, as Abrams observes, before the eighteenth century such writing was for the most part focused on the making of art—that is, on composing and performing. Writers offered advice to poets, musicians, painters, architects, and so forth on how to practice their craft. Beginning early in the eighteenth century, the emphasis in writings on the arts shifted from the artist who makes the art to the public who engages it.

This shift from the artist to the public was not sufficient to make the contemplation model dominant; for there are other ways in which the public engages works of art than contemplation. The altarpieces of the medieval Western church were not so much contemplated as caught up into the practices of Catholic piety; the pious knelt before them, lit candles in front of them. The eighteenth-century theorists could not have been ignorant of this devotional way of using painting and sculpture, but they paid it no attention. Art, they assumed and said, was for contemplation. Art belongs not to the active life but to the contemplative life—not to the *vita activa* but to the *vita contemplativa*. Abrams argues persuasively that this change in writing about art reflected changes in the actual use of art.

By using the phrase "*vita contemplativa*," I mean to suggest that the mode of engagement with art that came into prominence in eighteenth-century practice and theory amounted not just to an episode in the history of art but also to an episode in the history of that way of life that has periodically been praised and practiced ever since Plato—namely, the contemplative life. It was an episode in the history of the contemplative life that was of startling originality and daring, however. Plato had urged his readers to turn away from the sensory world and, by means of Reason, to contemplate the realm of Forms. By contrast, it was *perceptual* contemplation that the eighteenth-century theorists called for—the very thing Plato militated against.

The eighteenth-century theorists, by making the contemplation model dominant in their thinking about the arts, elevated the worth of perceptual contemplation—"contemplative engrossment," to borrow a phrase from Adorno[5]—above all other uses of art. That such "elevation" is what they were about becomes clear when we add one more ingredient to the mix. The eighteenth-century theorists urged a specific form of contemplation—not contemplation in general, but what they called "*disinterested* contemplation." The attempt to explain "disinterestedness" occupied theorists for the entire eighteenth century. Not until the end of the century, in Kant's *Critique of Judgment*, was it finally given a satisfactory explanation—though in the interests of full disclosure I should add that some hold that not even Kant succeeded in explaining the idea.

The Grand Modern Narrative of the Arts slowly emerged to explain the changes that occurred in the practices of the arts among the bourgeousie in eighteenth-century Western Europe and the corresponding changes in how writers about the arts conceptualized those changes in practice. It is a narrative of progress. The story of the eighteenth-century revolution in the arts might have been told as the story of yet one more alteration in the ancient and enduring social practices of music, painting, poetry, and the like. That, in my view, is how the story should be told; but the story of the revolution, as the Grand Narrative tells it, is the story of art finally being liberated and coming into its own in the eighteenth century, after millennia of servitude.

The story goes like this: previously art was always in the service of something outside itself, especially religious and governmental officials and institutions. Now, in serving as object of disinterested contemplation, art is at long last coming into its own. That is to say, now at last people are moving away from engaging art for the sake of its utility for some extra-artistic purpose, and moving toward engaging it for its own sake. To treat a work of art as an object of disinterested contemplation is to treat it *as a work of art* rather than as an instrument for some extrinsic purpose. In being so engaged, art is both freed *from* extraneous influences and freed *for* following its own intrinsic dynamics. To be so engaged is the historical destiny of art. Henceforth the intrusion of political, economic, and religious considerations constitutes systemic distortion. Thus it is that Beardsley speaks, in the passage I quoted at the beginning, about the need to "protect" the arts "against the enormous political and economic forces that constantly threaten to control, distort, repress, or trivialize them."

Some have put the point by saying that art *qua* art is useless. In previous writings of mine, I charged those who speak thus with an astonishing lack of self-awareness. What they have to mean, I said, is not that art is literally useless, but that its use lies in its capacity for giving us aesthetic delight. The debate, I said, has to be seen not as a debate over use versus non-use, but as a debate over which use of art is best and noblest. Is there more value in using art for liturgical purposes, for example, or for the purpose of experiencing delight in disinterested contemplation? So also, in speaking of art as existing for its own sake they have to mean, I said, that art is for the sake of perceptual contemplation.

I now think I was wrong—wrong at least for many writers. What many of those meant who said that "art is useless" and that "art exists for its own sake" is that works of art have *objective intrinsic* excellence—just as Kant thought that persons have objective intrinsic excellence, and just as theists believe that God has objective intrinsic excellence. If that is one's thought, then disinterested contemplation will be seen as our way of becoming aware of, and acknowledging, the objective intrinsic excellence of the work of art. The alternative view that I was trying to impose is that it is the subjective experience of aesthetic delight that has intrinsic excellence, with works of art then having the derivative worth of being the objects of that intrinsically excellent subjective experience.[6]

Part of what led me to revise my opinion was an observation that M. H. Abrams makes in his essay, "Art-as-Such: The Sociology of Modern Aesthetics." Abrams notes the quite astonishing way in which writers about the arts in the eighteenth century took the language about God that one finds in the neo-Platonic and Augustinian contemplative traditions, and applied it to works of art. Karl Philipp Moritz, writing in 1785, provides him with some of his most vivid examples. Here are two passages that Abrams quotes from Moritz:

> In the contemplation of the beautiful object . . . I contemplate it as something which is *completed,* not in me, but *in its own self,* which therefore constitutes a whole in itself and affords me pleasure *for its own sake.*
>
> While the beautiful draws our attention exclusively to itself . . . we seem to lose ourselves in the beautiful object; and precisely this loss, this forgetfulness of self, is the highest degree of pure and disinterested pleasure that beauty grants us. In that moment we sacrifice our individual confined being to a kind of higher being. . . . Beauty in a work of art is not pure . . . until I contemplate it as something that has been brought forth entirely for its own sake, in order that it should be something complete in itself.[7]

And here is Wilhelm Wackenroder writing about the museum experience:

> Art galleries . . . ought to be temples where, in still and silent humility and in heart-lifting solitude, we may admire great artists as the highest among mortals . . . with long, steadfast contemplation of their works. . . . I compare the enjoyment of nobler works of art to *prayer.* . . . Works of art, in their way, no more fit into the common flow of life than does the thought of God. . . . That day is for me a sacred hol-

iday which . . . I devote to the contemplation of noble works of art.[8]

No doubt about it. The thought coming through in these passages is that works of art, at least those that serve well as objects of disinterested contemplation, are transcendent entities of intrinsic worth. Works of art are godlike and should be treated as such.

Whenever I present, as I have just now, the opening chapter in The Grand Modern Narrative of the Arts, I have Max Weber's theory of modernization ringing in my ears. It is commonly said that Weber got his notion of value-spheres from the neo-Kantianism of the mid-nineteenth century; and no doubt he did. But all the essential ideas were there already in the writings of the eighteenth-century art theorists. In art there is a distinct value—call it the aesthetic value. Up to the eighteenth century this value was seldom recognized and pursued in its own right. Now finally it is; and a distinct sphere of life is being organized around the recognition and pursuit of this value. Thereby the pursuit of this value is both liberated *from* its subservience to the pursuit of other values and liberated *for* shaping the sphere of the arts. If pursuit of this value is to be successful in shaping the sphere of the arts, life in the art world must be protected from systemic distortion by the intrusion of other and alien values—political, economic, religious, academic. That's Weber. And that's the eighteenth-century art theorists. The eighteenth-century art theorists were proto-Weberians.

In his book *Natural Supernaturalism,* M. H. Abrams tells the story of how this grand progressivist narrative became yet more grand by appropriating the social analysis of the Romantics. The early Romantics were the first great "secular" analysts and critics of modernity—that is, the first to believe that eighteenth-century social developments represented not just more of the same but something distinctly different, and then to give a secular analysis and critique of those developments. Their analysis was that the coming of modernity represents the loss of all the old social and psychological unities. Modernity is fragmentation—fragmentation of the old economic relationships, fragmentation of the old political arrangements, fragmentation of the church, fragmentation in the relation of knowers to nature. In that wonderful line from John Keats's long poem *Lamia,* cold philosophy (that is, natural science) will "unweave a rainbow." The subtext of Romanticism is disappointment—disappointment with the new science, with the new capitalist economy, with rational politics, with the institutional church.

But pervading the Romantic mentality is the additional conviction that when art is liberated from subservience to extraneous purposes and allowed to come into its own, then art and our disinterested engagement with art constitute an exception to the social dynamics of fragmentation. Such art and such engagement are socially other, socially transcendent. Essential to the very being of the work of art is that it be unified; in the very nature of the case, the artist unifies where modern society fragments. And intrinsic to that unity is a different form of rationality from the instrumental rationality that pervades society—purposeless rationality, intrinsic rationality. We the beholders come under the sway of that otherness.

Many accounts have been offered of the precise nature and import of the social otherness of art. But ever since the days of early Romanticism, one account of its import has been that in composing and presenting his work of unity and purposeless rationality, the artist both launches a critique against the fragmentation, rationalization, and oppression of social reality as we know it, and sets before us an image of an alternative reality; in that way, the work harbors the potential of being an agent of social reform. Art is salvific, redemptive, not by transporting us from this wicked world into a better world, as Moritz thought, but by harboring the prophetic/messianic potential of reforming this present wicked world. It is this latter conviction that lies behind the words I quoted from Marcuse at the beginning of this essay.

We have considered two overtly religious accounts of the nature and import of those works of art that reward or are produced for disinterested perceptual contemplation, the Moritz account, which holds that the work of art is like unto God in being of transcendent intrinsic worth, and the Marcuse account, which holds that the work of art, by its prophetic critique of our fallen world and its presentation of the messianic alternative, functions redemptively. A third overtly religious account sees the work of art neither as itself a transcendent object worthy of religious veneration, nor as a transcendent redemptive presence among us, but as making present to us the Transcendent when we engage it aesthetically. A fair number of artists of the modern and contemporary period have spoken of their own work this way: Robert Motherwell, Barnett Newman, perhaps Mark Rothko, perhaps Piet Mondriaan.

The theorist Clive Bell argued that all art, when contemplated aesthetically, puts us in the presence of the Transcendent. That this is Bell's view will come as a surprise to most students of aesthetics, since those who compose our standard anthologies of aesthetics seldom include those passages from Bell in which he gives his religious interpretation of art. Every student of aesthetics knows the following passage from Bell: "Art transports us from the world of man's activity to a world of aesthetic exaltation. For a moment we are shut off from human interests, our anticipations and memories are arrested; we are lifted above the stream of life."[9] And every student knows the passage in which Bell says that in aesthetic contemplation we "inhabit a world with an intense and peculiar significance of its own; that significance is unrelated to the significance of life."[10] These are just unusually eloquent statements of the Grand Narrative. What few students know about is Bell's religious account of art.

Why does pure form move us?, Bell asks. "Because it expresses the emotion of its creator," he says.[11] What sort of emotion is that? It is the emotion the artist feels upon seeing things in the world about him as pure forms. That is to say, the artist feels the aesthetic emotion when he views things in the world around him aesthetically, just as we feel the aesthetic emotion when we view works of art aesthetically. But to regard something as pure form is to see it as an end in itself, says Bell.[12] And now let me quote what Bell says about the import of seeing something as an end in itself, whether that be a work of art or a thing in the world:

> . . . when we consider anything as an end in itself we
> become aware of that in it which is of greater
> moment than any qualities it may have acquired
> from keeping company with human beings. Instead
> of recognising its accidental and conditioned impor-
> tance, we become aware of its essential reality, of the
> God in everything, of the universal in the particular,
> of the all-pervading rhythm. Call it by what name
> you will, the thing that I am talking about is that
> which lies behind the appearance of all things—that

which gives to all things their individual significance, the thing in itself, the ultimate reality.[13]

Why have most anthologizers excluded this part of Bell's book from their collections? A clue lies in the attitude toward religion prevalent in the twentieth-century academy.

Religion has come to seem irrational and oppressive— not accidentally so, but in its very nature. As will be clear from the foregoing, the Romantics had no hostility toward religion per se. Quite the contrary. It was institutional religion that they turned their backs on; such religion seemed to them part and parcel of the fragmentation, rationalization, and oppression of the modern social world. But to our twentieth-century academics, Bell's pantheism seems no more rational than theism. So a vast expurgation of religion from the Western artistic and intellectual tradition has taken place. We will include Clive Bell in our anthologies, but just the purely philosophical part, not the religious part. We will treat Vincent van Gogh in our histories of modern art; but we will treat him simply as an important development in the history of Western stylistics, ignoring all the stuff in his letters to Theo about painting God in the sun. Large audiences will listen with rapt attention to Olivier Messiaen's *Vingt regards sur l'enfant Jésus;* but our critics will ignore the theological program of Christian mysticism that lies behind Messiaen's composition and deal just with the sounds as such. The attitude throughout is that religion, though often there, is not worth taking note of. It is thought to be an irrational addendum that may as well be ignored.

Lest you think that I as a philosopher am being unfairly judgmental of art critics and historians, let me hasten to add that the same has been true for historians of philosophy. The great modern philosophers have been treated as if they were either purely secular thinkers or as if their religious thoughts made no difference to their philosophy. Just recently there has been something of a backlash. Over the past decade, for example, a considerable number of books have appeared arguing that John Locke's philosophy is so intimately intertwined with his Christian conviction that the philosophy cannot be understood apart from that conviction.[14] So perhaps the times are changing.

If the classic secularization thesis were true—that modernization brings secularization in its wake—then I would presumably be sensible to regard the religious component in our intellectual and artistic culture as a relic of the adolescence of our species and do what we can to excise it, conceding that often, in cutting it out, quite a bit of the philosophy of art goes out with it. But I gather from my friends in sociology that the secularization thesis is now pretty much dead. To see why, one only has to look around—not just at society in general but at what is happening in the high arts. Arvo Pärt, John Tavener, James Macmillan, Sophia Gubaidulina, Henryck Górecki, Olivier Messiaen—these are among our most popular present-day composers. In each case, explicitly religious compositions constitute a large part of their body of work. And the religion tends not to be mystical, but more or less traditionally Christian.

Not all who embrace the Grand Narrative would be willing to endorse any of the three religious accounts of the import of disinterested contemplation that I have cited. R. G. Collingwood, for example, would not. The three central components of the Grand Narrative are the two Weber-like theses—that art comes into its own when our mode of engagement is disinterested perceptual contemplation and that such engagement should now be freed to follow out its own intrinsic dynamics—and the Romantic thesis, that art created for such engagement represents an alternative to the fragmentation, rationalization, and oppression pervading and shaping modern society. On these three components, there has been near-universal agreement among philosophers of art of the modern period. By contrast, there has never been consensus on what it is about disinterested contemplation that is of fundamental worth. So there have been polemics, sometimes heated. Adorno, for example, was biting, even vicious, in his attack on the aestheticist account in his *Aesthetic Theory;* Gadamer, though more measured in his rhetoric, was just as firm in Part One of his *Truth and Method.* But these are family quarrels; it never occurred to Adorno or Gadamer to question the Grand Narrative itself. Recently some have spoken up in defense of beauty in art; they too conduct their argument within the confines of the Grand Narrative.

The point I want to keep before us, though, is this: hotly contested though the significance of disinterested contemplation and its objects has been by those who embrace the Grand Narrative, what is truly remarkable is how often, for two-and-a-half centuries now, one or another of the three religious themes I have cited gets sounded. Even the ever-restrained Beardsley is right on the edge of overtly religious language. The Grand Narrative, though it does not require religious legitimation, has certainly invited it.

I submit that the conclusion to be drawn from the studies of the past twenty-five years is that we must give up the Grand Modern Narrative of the Arts—not give up the Kantian or Beardsleyan aesthetic version in favor, say, of the Hegelian or Heideggerian alethic version, but give up the Narrative itself. The narrative flies in the face of the evidence. The artist does not transcend our social condition, nor does the art she produces. Art is racist, not always but often, and sexist, colonialist, elitist, nationalist, fascist—you name it. Not only is it all these things in its content; it also functions socially as an instrument of oppression and exploitation. It always has. The pyramids were not tossed up in a frenzy of voluntary exuberance. I, as a Calvinist of sorts, am constantly surprised that anyone would find this surprising. What else would one expect? And works of art are often not unified; they are full of gaps, contradictions, *aporia*.

If the Romantic-analysis component of the Grand Narrative cannot be upheld, what about the Weber-like components? Are those acceptable? One of the Weber-like theses is that the art world comprises a distinct differentiated sphere of life that is properly determined by its own distinct artistic value; and that when things are going properly, life in the art world is shaped exclusively by this artistic value and not by political, economic, and religious values. Is this true? Is it true that in so far as life in the art world is shaped by these latter values, life in the art world is systemically distorted?

It is true that the art world constitutes an identifiable formation in our society; and it is true that there is such a formation because a considerable number of us find value in the engrossed contemplation of works of art. That is the value around which this sphere of life is oriented, difficult and controversial though it has proved to be to explain just what that value is. But that said, what must then at once be added is that the practices and institutions that go to make up this art world are shaped by political, economic, religious, and technological developments. How could it be otherwise? High art music requires concert halls and orchestras; the construction and maintenance of concert halls, and the maintenance of symphony orchestras, require money; and money is always allocated among competing recipients. Economics and politics are internal to the arts. In short, it is profoundly misguided to talk about autonomous, self-normed, development.

So what, lastly, about the other Weber-like thesis, the progressivist, Whiggish claim that disinterested perceptual contemplation represents art finally come into its own—that is, represents the value *intrinsic* to art finally freed to shape our engagement with the arts? This is the bottom strand of the entire narrative; if this goes, it all goes.

Well, when does an artifact come into its own? Take a chair, for example; when does a chair come into its own? Presumably when it is used as it was meant to be used by maker or distributor, that is, when somebody sits on it. There are lots of chairs on display in the art museums of the world. But when a chair is merely looked at, it is not coming into its own. Not coming into its own *as a chair.*

Now consider works of art—by which I mean, products of one or another of those social practices of making that you and I call "the fine arts," works of music, works of fiction, two-dimensional visual designs and representations, and the like. From this whole array let us single out, say, liturgical art; and from liturgical art let us single out, say, hymns. When does a hymn come into its own? Does it come into its own when it serves as an object of engrossed contemplation? Obviously not. A hymn comes into its own when the members of a religious community all together sing it so as to express their praise, their confession, their thanksgiving. You see the point. Some art comes into its own when it becomes the object of engrossed contemplation; most art does not come into its own that way.

I see only one last line of defense for the person who wants to hang on to something at least of the second Weber-like thesis. Let it be granted that the arts have always been multifunctional; they come into their own in a multiplicity of different ways. That explains why they sink so deeply into our human existence. But could it be that the worth of engaging works of art as objects of engrossed contemplation, whatever that worth may be, is superior to the worth of any other way of engaging the arts? Could it be that there is greater worth in listening to a performance of Stravinsky's *Mass* in the concert hall than in participating in a religious service in which his *Mass* serves as the music of the liturgy? We are now at rock bottom in the argument, where there is little else to do than declare one's own convictions. As for me, I see no reason to believe that listening to Stravinsky's *Mass* in the concert hall is of more worth than participating in a religious service for which it is the liturgical music.

How do we proceed from here? Or is there no proceeding? Must we learn to live among the shards of the Grand Narrative? I think we can do better than that. The basic move to make is to give up the Whiggish narrative of art as finally coming into its own in the eighteenth century when disinterested contemplation of works of art became prominent. The eighteenth-century revolution represented a radical development in the age-old practices of the arts. It represented no more than that—though also no less. What you and I classify as the arts have always undergone changes, sometimes wrenching, sometimes gentle, sometimes in response to developments more or less internal to the arts, sometimes in response to developments more or less external. The eighteenth-century revolution was one of the more radical alterations in the history of the arts. But it is a mistake to think of developments prior to the eighteenth century as all leading up to this climax of liberation.

May it be that you and I are now standing on the cusp of the decline of the eighteenth-century development? May it be that engrossed contemplation of works of art is on the way to becoming less and less important to us, and that the institutions built up to support this mode of engagement are about to go into decline? Is that the significance of the difficulties that symphony orchestras are presently experiencing? I doubt it. There are too many counter-indications: the number of new museums built in recent years, for example.

But if it should turn out that we are standing on the cusp of the decline of the eighteenth-century development, that implies nothing about the fate of the arts as such. The fate of the arts is not to be identified with the fate of art meant for engrossed contemplation. If we are talking about the fate of the arts in general, not to worry. Art is too indispensable for too much of what we find worth doing to be in danger of disappearing.

Suppose we discard the Grand Narrative and do our thinking about the arts along the lines I have suggested. What changes might we expect? I have given here only the vaguest glimpse of what such an alternative way of thinking would look like, but perhaps we have seen enough to draw a few tentative conclusions.

I think the changes within the arts themselves would not be all that great. There would be some shifts in esteem; no longer would artists who produce liturgical art, urban art, memorial art, and so forth, be viewed as slumming it. And no doubt alterations in esteem would have a ripple effect. But mainly the changes would come in how we study and think about the arts. We would begin to explore those many ways of engaging the arts that have been neglected by philosophy of art of the modern period. Let me give a few examples.

I consider the French artist Georges Rouault, who did most of his work between the two World Wars, to be one of the great painters and printmakers of the first half of the twentieth century. Rouault is not widely esteemed nowadays, mainly, so far as I can tell, because critics and historians who adopt the secularizing approach find the religious component in his work too up-front. But suppose we broaden our perspective. Suppose we approach Rouault not just with the category of art for disinterested contemplation but with a category that goes virtually unrecognized in philosophy of art of the modern period—the category of *memorial art*. Memorial art is art meant to keep alive and honor the memory of some person or event from the past. Fundamental to Christianity, as to Judaism, Islam, and Buddhism, is remembering certain numinous persons and events; in the case of Christianity and Buddhism, one of the principle ways in which that is accomplished is by means of pictorial and sculptural art. Then it becomes clear at once that along with whatever else he was doing, Rouault was producing memorial art. And the challenge for the theorist is to think through what it is for a work of art to function as memorial art, in contrast to functioning as an object of engrossed contemplation.

Once we have the category of memorial art in hand, then it will at once be obvious that memorial art is by no means confined to the remembering done by such religions as Christianity and Buddhism. New York City has recently been engaged in a fascinating public discussion of memorial art—a discussion, specifically, about the form to be taken by the art located at Ground Zero memorializing the victims of 9/11. And among the best-known works of art produced in the last quarter of the twentieth century is Maya Lin's Vietnam Memorial.

One of the many things that fascinate me about memorial art is the fact that the standard mode of engagement with works such as the Vietnam Memorial is not contemplation but touching and kissing—which is also how the Eastern Orthodox engage their icons. The Orthodox do not contemplate their icons. When certain icons find their way into our museums, you and I contemplate them; we allow ourselves to be engrossed by their aesthetic qualities. But the Orthodox kiss their icons, bow to them, light candles before them. In short, they venerate them. You will not find an analysis of veneration in any philosophy of art of the modern period.[15]

Move from memorial art to liturgical art. A number of quite different things go on when art is used within the liturgy and its context. One thing that has for some time intrigued me is that the worshippers take onto their own lips poetry composed years earlier, sometimes centuries and even millennia earlier, so as thereby to express their own thoughts and feelings. The words of the poetry become their own words. This, too, is a mode of engagement with art that, to the best of my knowledge, is nowhere acknowledged in our modern philosophies of art. For, of course, it is distinctly different from perceptual contemplation. One does not contemplate the poetry, nor does one recite it; one appropriates it.

I could go on in this vein; urban art, the art of political resistance, ceremonial and celebrative art—all of them enjoy little recognition in philosophy of art of the modern period. But I will stop. I hope I have offered a glimpse of the vast and fascinating terrain that beckons when, no longer fixated on art for contemplation, we are open to exploring the manifold ways in which we human beings engage works of art.

An important question remains. Suppose we discard the Grand Narrative and think of art along the alternative lines I have suggested. How then should we appraise those three types of religious significance attached to art over the past two-and-a-half centuries? Granted that art is not as such socially other; both the works and their makers participate in our fallenness. May it nonetheless be the case that here and there, now and then, works of transcendent intrinsic worth emerge? Or that, here and there, now and then, the Transcendent is manifested? Or that, here and there, now and then, works emerge that offer a critique of social reality and function redemptively? Can these modest theses be affirmed?

The claim that works of art are of transcendent intrinsic worth smacks to me of idolatry. They may be of intrinsic worth; I rather think they are. But not of such intrinsic worth as to be worthy of worship. They may, though, sometimes manifest the Transcendent. This is not a thesis I reject—though I have never known how to articulate it sufficiently to be able to appraise it. The third thesis is the one that attracts me.

It is my experience that injustice seldom has an energizing effect until it acquires a human face and a human voice. That face and voice may be physically present before one, but they may also be re-presented, in fiction and film. The novels of Nadine Gordimer and J. M. Coetzee, to name only two examples, gave a face and a voice to the injustice of the Afrikaaner regime, along with hints of how things might be instead. In so doing, they played a redemptive function. So, too, did Harriet Beecher Stowe's novel, *Uncle Tom's Cabin.* Apparently nobody today reads Stowe's novel for its purely aesthetic qualities; perhaps nobody ever did. Yet it played an important redemptive role in mid-nineteenth-century America. One does not have to prove the intrinsic social otherness of art and artists; all one need do is observe.

The point is that works of art can play a redemptive role even when they bear the traces of nationalism, sexism, racism, whatever. The Hebrew prophets were no doubt sexist, nationalist, all of that and more. Yet their word proved redemptive. So it is with art, now and then, here and there.

Notes

1. Monroe C. Beardsley, "Art and Its Cultural Context," *The Aesthetic Point of View: Selected Essays,* ed. Michael J. Wreen

and Donald M. Callen (Ithaca: Cornell University Press, 1982), 352.

2. Herbert Marcuse, *The Aesthetic Dimension* (Boston: Beacon, 1978), 6–8.

3. Paul Oskar Kristeller, *Renaissance Thought II* (New York: Harper Torchbooks, 1965).

4. Both are to be found in Abrams' collection, *Doing Things with Texts: Essays in Criticism and Critical Theory,* ed. Michael Fischer (New York: Norton, 1989).

5. Theodor Adorno, *Aesthetic Theory,* trans. C. Lenhardt (London: Routledge and Kegan Paul, 1984), 252.

6. This clearly is the view of some writers—for example, Monroe Beardsley, in the essays collected in Part I of his *The Aesthetic Point of View,* ed. Michael J. Wreen and Donald M. Callen (Ithaca: Cornell University Press, 1982).

7. Abrams, "Art-as-Such: The Sociology of Modern Aesthetics," *Doing Things with Texts: Essays in Criticism and Critical Theory,* ed. Michael Fischer (New York: Norton, 1989), 156.

8. Abrams, "Art-as-Such: The Sociology of Modern Aesthetics," 157.

9. Clive Bell, *Art* (London: Chatto & Windus, 1914), 27.

10. Bell, *Art,* 28.

11. Bell, *Art,* 43.

12. Bell, *Art,* 45.

13. Bell, *Art,* 54.

14. The most recent example is Jeremy Waldron's *God, Locke, and Equality: Christian Foundations in Locke's Political Thought* (Cambridge: Cambridge University Press, 2002).

15. I have discussed memorial art in two articles: "Why Philosophy of Art Cannot Handle Kissing, Touching, and Crying," *The Journal of Aesthetics and Art Criticism,* Winter 2003, *61*(1), 17–27; and "The Art of Remembering," *The Cresset,* June 1992, LV.7B, 20–28.

Andy Crouch is editorial director of the Christian Vision Project at Christianity Today International and is working on a book about Christian cultural responsibility. He lives in Swarthmore, Pennsylvania.

Michael P. Foley has a doctorate in systematic theology from Boston College and is the author of *Why Do Catholics Eat Fish on Friday? The Catholic Origin to Just About Everything.* He is assistant professor of Patristics in the Great Texts Program at Baylor University.

Mark Galli is managing editor of *Christianity Today* magazine. He is the author most recently of *Francis of Assisi and His World.*

William Griffin is a writer, translator, and editor. Among his recent books are a new translation of Thomas à Kempis's *The Imitation of Christ* and a Chesterton anthology, *G. K. Chesterton: Essential Writings.* He lives in Alexandria, Louisiana, with his wife and fellow writer, Emilie.

Amy Laura Hall, a minister of the United Methodist Church, teaches theological ethics at Duke University. She is the author of *Kierkegaard and the Treachery of Love.* Her essay in this volume was first presented as the O. P. Kretzmann Lecture at Valparaiso University.

Richard Lischer teaches at Duke Divinity School. He is the author of *Open Secrets: A Memoir of Faith and Discovery* and the editor of *The Company of Preachers: Wisdom on Preaching, Augustine to the Present.*

Paul Marshall is senior fellow at Freedom House's Center for Religious Freedom. Among his recent books are *Islam at the Crossroads* and *God and the Constitution.*

Frederica Mathewes-Green is the author most recently of *The Open Door: Entering the Sanctuary of Icons and Prayer.* She is a commentator on NPR, and her movie reviews appear regularly in a variety of publications.

Bill McKibben is the author of many books, including *Enough: Staying Human in an Engineered Age* and *Wandering Home: A Long Walk Across America's Most Hopeful Landscape.* He is scholar-in-residence at Middlebury College.

Richard J. Mouw is president of Fuller Seminary. Among his recent books are *He Shines in All That's Fair: Culture and Common Grace* and *Calvinism in the Las Vegas Airport: Making Connections in Today's World.*

Richard John Neuhaus is editor-in-chief of *First Things.* Among his many books are *The Catholic Moment: The Paradox of the Church in the Postmodern World* and *The Naked Public Square: Religion and Democracy in America.*

Mark Noll is McManis Professor of Christian Thought at Wheaton College. Among his many books are *America's God: From Jonathan Edwards to Abraham Lincoln* and *The Scandal of the Evangelical Mind.*

Virginia Stem Owens is a novelist, essayist, and poet. Her most recent book, written with David Clinton Owens, is *Living Next Door to the Death House.*

Stephen Prothero is chairman of the Department of Religion at Boston University. He is the author most recently of *American Jesus: How the Son of God Became a National Icon.*

Gideon Strauss is the research and education director of the Christian Labour Association of Canada and editor of *Comment,* the journal of the Work Research Foundation.

Daniel Taylor is professor of English at Bethel College. Among his books are *The Myth of Certainty* and, most recently, *In Search of Sacred Places: Looking for Wisdom on Celtic Holy Islands.*

August Turak is a lifetime spiritual seeker and businessman who has studied under such diverse teachers as Richard Rose, an American Zen master; Lou Mobley, the founder of the IBM Executive School; and Father Christian Carr, OCSO, the former Abbot of Mepkin Abbey monastery. In 1989 he founded the Self Knowledge Symposium Foundation, a nonprofit organization dedicated to encouraging students to develop their own personal, moral, and spiritual values in order to pursue a meaningful and authentic life. His essay in this volume was the winner in the John Templeton Foundation's "Power of Purpose" worldwide essay competition.

Paul J. Willis is professor of English at Westmont College in Santa Barbara, California. His most recent collection of poems is *How to Get There*. With David Starkey, he is the editor of *In a Fine Frenzy: Poets Respond to Shakespeare*.

John Wilson is the editor of *Books & Culture* and an editor at large for *Christianity Today* magazine.

Lauren F. Winner is the author of *Girl Meets God: On the Path to a Spiritual Life* and *Real Sex: The Naked Truth About Chastity*.

Gregory Wolfe is publisher and editor of *Image: A Journal of the Arts & Religion*. Among his books are *Intruding Upon the Timeless: Meditations on Art, Faith, and Mystery* and *Malcolm Muggeridge: A Biography*.

Nicholas Wolterstorff is Noah Porter Professor Emeritus of Philosophical Theology, Yale University. Among his many books are *Art and Action: Toward a Christian Aesthetic* and *Lament for a Son*.

"Odd Job" by Richard Lischer. First published in *The Christian Century*, April 6, 2004. Copyright © 2004 by Richard Lischer. Reprinted by permission of Richard Lischer.

"Islamic Counter-Reformation" by Paul Marshall. First published in *First Things*, August-September 2004. Copyright © 2004 by *First Things*. Reprinted by permission of *First Things*.

"The Meaning of Christ's Suffering" by Frederica Mathewes-Green. First published in *Books & Culture*, March-April 2004. A different version of this essay appeared at Beliefnet.com. Copyright © 2004 by Frederica Mathewes-Green. Reprinted by permission of Frederica Mathewes-Green.

"High Fidelity" by Bill McKibben. First published in *The Christian Century*, March 23, 2004. Copyright © 2004 by Bill McKibben. Reprinted by permission of Bill McKibben.

"Confessions of a Traveling Calvinist" by Richard J. Mouw. Taken from *Calvinism in the Las Vegas Airport*. Copyright © 2004 by Richard J. Mouw. Reprinted by permission of The Zondervan Corporation.

"The Persistence of the Catholic Moment" by Richard John Neuhaus. First published in *First Things*, February 2003. Copyright © 2003 by *First Things*. Reprinted by permission of *First Things*.

"Thanksgiving at Fair Acres" by Virginia Stem Owens. First published in *Christianity Today*, November 2000. Copy-